Julie **Kniveton**
Angela **Llanas**

Teacher's Edition

Macmillan Education
Between Towns Road, Oxford OX4 3PP
A division of Macmillan Publishers Limited

Companies and representatives throughout the world

Bounce Now Level 3 Teacher's Edition (English)

ISBN 978-0-230-42010-6

Text, design and illustration © Macmillan Publishers Limited 2011
Written by Maria del Carmen Fernández
Adapted by Lorena Peimbert
Translated by Alison Warner
Big Book Builder Teacher's Notes written by Angela Llanas

First published 2011

Original design by Ben Cracknell Studios
Page make-up by Cambridge Publishing Management Limited
Cover design by Roberto Martínez
Cover Photography by Gerardo Reyes

Student's Book Credits:
Text © Julie Kniveton and Angela Llanas 2011
Designed by Ben Cracknell Studios, Designers Collective, Fusion
Enterprises, Neil Straker Creative, Vector Creative Solutions
Original design Ben Cracknell Studios
Page make-up by Cambridge Publishing Management Limited
Illustrated by Beccy Blake; Joe Boddy; Creative Design Limited; Richard
Duszczak; Robin Edmonds; Javier Joaquin; Kim and James (Just for Laffs);
David Le Jars (Just for Laffs); Sean Longcroft (Just for Laffs); Ainslie
Macleod; Sean Parks; Peter Richardson; Anthony Rule; Phil Starr.
Picture Research by Gill Metcalfe
Cover design by Roberto Martínez
Commissioned photographs by Dean Ryan

The authors and publishers would like to thank the following for permission
to reproduce their photographs:
Alamy/ Best View Stock p75(br), Alamy/ Horizon International Images
Limited p35(br), Alamy/ Jon Arnold Images p67(r), Alamy/ Robert W
Ginn p35(bl), Alamy/ Vibe Images p19(tr); **Bananastock** p43(bl);
Brand X p11(tr, cr, br); Comstock pp43(tr), 59(cr); Corbis p35(cr), p51;
Getty pp11(c), 27(tr), 35(cl), 59(tl, tm, bl, bml, br), Getty/ Photographer's
Choice/ Barbara Peacock p19(m), Getty/ Riser/ Terry Williams p67(l),
Getty/ Stone/ Terry Vine p75(t); **Image Source** pp43(br), 59(tr);
Istock p43(tl); **Macmillan**/ Paul Bricknell pp11(l), 27(tl); *Macmillan
Australia* pp27(m), 59(bmr); **Photoalto** p35(tl); **Photodisc** p35(tr);
Stockbyte p67(m); **Up the Resolution** p59 (cl, cm)

These materials may contain links for third party websites. We have no
control over, and are not responsible for, the contents of such third party
websites. Please use care when accessing them.

Printed and bound in Thailand

2015 2014 2013 2012 2011
10 9 8 7 6 5 4 3 2 1

Contents

Introduction

For the student

Student's Book
The Student's Book contains illustrated vocabulary and grammar presentations. New language is practiced and consolidated through a range of contexts, including stories, songs and manual activities relating to the real world. The final section of the book contains Home Study Worksheets, which are exercises to practice the language learned in class.

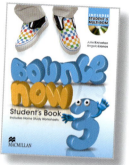

Student's Multi-ROM
The Multi-ROM for each level offers entertaining and interactive games to practice spelling, dictation and vocabulary; it also contains all the audio tracks used in class so students can review the lessons and do the listening exercises.

Activity Resource Book
The Activity Resource Book provides students with activities and suggestions for each song, and templates for the manual activities suggested in the Student's Book for vocabulary practice.

For the teacher

Teacher's Edition
It shows the pages of the Student's Book and provides answers and clear and accurate notes for each lesson. It also offers activities to develop competencies, as well as suggestions for homework and continuous assessment.

Big Book Builders
Each book contains 18 posters, an illustrated dictionary (levels 1–4), and an audio program.

Teacher's Multi-ROM
The Teacher's Multi-ROM contains a fully projectable version of both the student's book and the Big Book Builder. It also offers integrated audio and interactive tools, with all the audio tracks required for each level, plus a monthly program to help teachers plan their lessons.

Assessment Pack
This pack contains information on all the assessments for each level and unit; it also contains assessment tables to record the results of the language assessments, the global assessments and the self assessments.

Features and Skills

Bounce Now icons

This icon appears whenever the Teacher's Multi-ROM contains a listening activity.

BLM 1

A *Word window* appears in Lesson 1 of each unit, providing an example of the new word and giving the relevant page number in the Activity Resource Book.

Students can reproduce the word cards for personal use or for review games. The different colors represent the grammar learned. Red is used for nouns and blue for verbs. This resource can be used whenever the teacher thinks the class needs additional grammar review.

The *Today's grammar* board summarizes the lesson's new structure and offers ideas about how to organize information on the board.

This icon appears when students need to adapt the language learned through oral exercises.

This icon features in the *Bounce around* lessons (Lesson 8 of each unit), which provide students with the opportunity to practice the unit's new language and integrate it into other areas of the curriculum.

This icon represents the *Write about* lessons in which students practice and develop writing skills through texts and parallel exercises.

This icon appears when the activity involves reviewing language from oral exercises.

Competencies developed with *Bounce Now*

Act: Helps students develop an understanding of the importance of having an overall awareness and respect for other people's ideas and beliefs.

Collaborate: Helps students work in teams and communicate their ideas and experiences.

Learn: Helps students develop learning strategies and organize previously acquired knowledge as well as the new skills they are learning.

Me: Helps students develop an awareness of their own tastes, feelings and ideas and actively participate in the learning/teaching process through self assessment.

Think: Helps students develop critical thinking skills.

Component Analysis

Contents of the Student's Book

The activities in the *Word window* provide students with an opportunity to reuse the vocabulary in a visual manner; these activities can also be used to decorate the classroom's walls or to take home to show to families. The templates for each lesson in the Activity Resource Book can be used by students to color and cut out. These templates can also be used for an illustrated dictionary (*pictionary*).

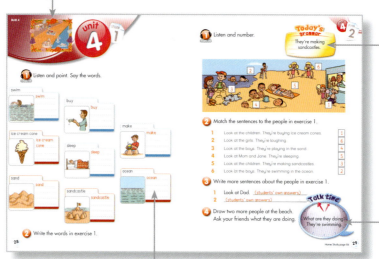

New grammar is summarized on the *Today's grammar* board.

Students can customize new language within a controlled and informal context.

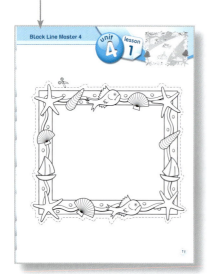

New vocabulary is presented with a visual reference as well as the written word, and students can hear the spoken word via the Student's Multi-ROM. Lesson 1 of each unit presents new vocabulary, which is then reviewed in the following lessons in a range of contexts. Students can copy the word cards to use them as a point of reference or for the role-play activities. Nouns will have a red border and verbs a blue one.

Students develop writing skills through a wide range of texts. Parallel texts provide context and can be used for review activities.

Students constantly review previously learned language through the *Bounce back* exercises.

In each unit, lively songs provide a more practical context for the new language. The Activity Resource Book contains a page with additional activities for each song.

All the songs, stories and a number of entertaining games are available on the Student's Multi-ROM for students to enjoy again.

Information to easily identify the lesson's homework task.

Bounce around Lessons

Lesson 8 of each unit links the vocabulary the students have learned to other contexts such as math, science, social sciences, geography, etc. to help them understand the reality of the language in a practical and entertaining way.

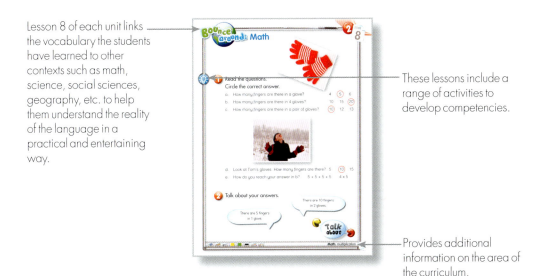

These lessons include a range of activities to develop competencies.

Provides additional information on the area of the curriculum.

Task program in *Bounce Now*

1 Home Study Worksheets
The worksheets include a space where teachers or students can write down the instructions (given in the Teacher's Edition). This will allow parents to support their children at home and keep a record of the work carried out.

Students can practice the vocabulary they have learned in class by doing the exercises.

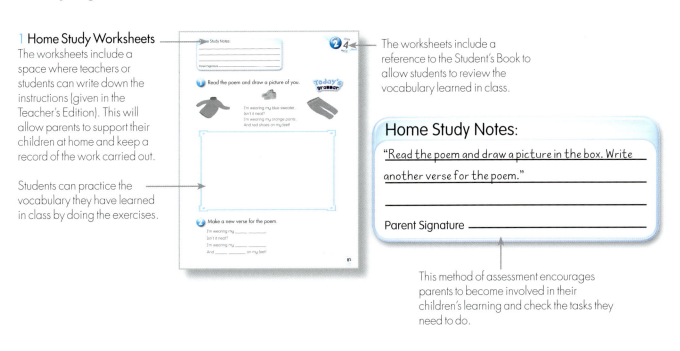

The worksheets include a reference to the Student's Book to allow students to review the vocabulary learned in class.

Home Study Notes:

"Read the poem and draw a picture in the box. Write another verse for the poem."

Parent Signature _____

This method of assessment encourages parents to become involved in their children's learning and check the tasks they need to do.

2 Multi-ROM task
Lessons 1 and 5 in each unit offer a Multi-ROM task so students can practice the vocabulary in the form of interactive games.

Multi-ROM task   Student's Multi-ROM

Ask students to listen to the song *Months are fun to say!*, track 04, at home until they have learned it by heart.

3 Listening task
Multi-ROM listening tasks allow students to review the songs or stories they have learned.

Contents of the Teacher's Edition

Quick reference to the materials needed for the lesson.

An easy and practical way of assessing the attitudes and values of students in order to produce the thought-provoking exercises required for an all-round education.

Instructions for the manual *Word window* activities.

The icons allow teachers to easily identify the type of tasks in each lesson, as well as the notes students need to write in their Home Study Worksheets.

Suggestions for entertaining warm-ups to start the lesson.

Each lesson contains two additional activities to review the language learned.

Suggestions on how to use the skills as a foundation for learning.

Suggestions about how to use the Teacher's Multi-ROM to plan interactive and different classes, with reference to either the Student's Book or the Big Book Builders.

Teachers are also given instructions on how and when to use the Big Book Builders during the class.

Provides the answers to the exercises in the Student's Book.

What is a *Bounce Now* Big Book Builder?

The *Bounce Now* Big Book Builder contains posters and an illustrated dictionary for each of the series' topics. The words in the pictionary are extremely useful and can be used every day. Each Big Book Builder contains 18 topic posters linked to the subjects explored in *Bounce Now*. The Big Book Builder is easy to carry around and show in class, and can be used for a wide range of classroom activities such as:

- Presenting and reviewing vocabulary in the correct context

- Developing a wider vocabulary

- Providing an entertaining lesson

- Encouraging work in pairs

- Spelling activities

- Exploring the relationship between the contents and the other subjects of the study program

- Performing language and memory games

- Exploring values

- Working interactively using the Teacher's Multi-ROM.

The *Bounce Now* Big Book Builder can be used at various times during the unit to present, practice and review language.

Each Big Book Builder contains:

- Topical headings to assist categorization

- Colored topic posters showing the vocabulary in different contexts

- Pictures in alphabetic order to help students isolate each element and identify it within a given context

- Two additional activities for extra language practice

Three types of assessment in *Bounce Now*

Assessing students is a challenging issue. It is important to understand that it is easier to assess students if you consider them as complete human beings, and focus on the skills, attitudes, aptitudes and knowledge they need to acquire through the educational process. This is the basis for learning through the acquisition of competencies.

In response to these educational requirements, *Bounce Now* suggests three types of assessment:

 ## Global Assessment

Teachers can assess performance, skills and the abilities students are developing across the units and guide them using the criteria presented at the start of each Lesson 1. Teachers must complete the record sheet and observe students to ensure that, at the end of the unit, the student's performance can be assessed. It is important to deal with students who need help and inform their parents, if necessary, about how they can help their children at home.

Global Assessment

Global assessment focuses on children's **attitudes** and **values** in their English class as well as their **Learning abilities**. Copy the Global Assessment Indicators for the level you teach, and your students' names into the Global Assessment Chart on page 5. Make a copy of the chart for each unit of the book (9 copies in total). At the end of each unit, evaluate your students according to the criteria below.

Grade	Global Assessment 1	Global Assessment 2	Global Assessment 3	Global Assessment 4
1	Participates in class activities	Follows instructions	Looks after school material	Is friendly with classmates
2	Pays attention in class	Takes care with school work	Collaborates in group work	Expresses ideas and opinions respectfully
3	Collaborates in team work	Values the presentation of school work	Respects the class rules	Shows interest in learning
4	Shows interest in the opinions of classmates	Give opinions and asks for help	Asks questions in class when unsure	Respects others' opinions
5	Works well in teams	Hands in homework	Brings all material to class	Is respectful and collaborates with classmates and teachers
6	Accepts input and suggestions from others	Hands in homework	Participates actively in class	Is respectful when expressing ideas and opinions

During the lessons, try to make time to monitor the children in your class while they are doing different activities. You will need more than one lesson to do this for large classes. To help you assess the children's overall performance after each unit, use these criteria: **ALWAYS**, **SOMETIMES**, and **NEVER**.

 ## Language Assessment

Teachers can check how much their students have learned using these short exercises that integrate all the elements acquired during the unit.

It is important that this assessment is always performed under the same conditions: on the same day, at the same time, in the same place, to ensure the test is truly reliable.

Language Assessment

This is designed to evaluate children's **comprehension** and **usage** of the new **Language**. For each unit in the Student's Book, there is a photocopiable **Language Assessment Sheet** in this pack. Use them after the children have completed the activities in the Student's Book and the Home Study pages for each unit.

Each Language Assessment has a total of 10 points. The activities are designed to reflect the language and the type of activities the children have seen and practiced in the unit.

Try to create the same conditions for each assessment.

1. Do the test in the same place at the same time each month.
2. Allow 30 minutes for each test.
3. Assess the children's language, not their ability to draw or write neatly.

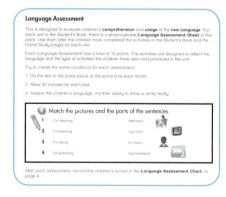

Match the pictures and the parts of the sentences.

1 I'm cleaning — television
2 I'm listening — my room
3 I'm doing — to music
4 I'm watching — my homework

After each assessment, record the children's scores in the **Language Assessment Chart** on page 4.

 ## Self Assessment

Students can participate in the learning/teaching process by self assessing their own performance throughout the unit. In this way, students can assess their strengths and weaknesses to help them improve throughout the course. It is important to encourage students to perform this exercise as honestly as possible, and jointly set out specific objectives to work on during the next unit; and it is important to monitor that the objectives are actually met to see an improvement in the student.

Self-Assessment

It is important for children to reflect on their own progress to understand that learning is a process. At the end of each unit, draw the chart below on the board and ask the children to copy it in their notebooks. Have them reflect on themselves and their English classes this month.

Month: _____

I always try my best.		
I always do my homework.		
I respect my classmates.		
I think my English is ...		

10 ideas for using *Bounce Now* Big Book Builder levels 3 and 4:

 Picture Walk: Show students the Topic Poster, but cover the title. Get students to guess the title, for example, *The Concert*. Point to different items on the picture and get students to say the words aloud.

 Alphabet Brainstorm: Show the Topic Poster to the group and ask students to say aloud the different things they can see. Write the words down on the board as they are saying them, or ask some of the students to write them. Students are then to write down the words in alphabetical order in their notebooks. Compare the students' list with the list of words in the illustrated dictionary.

 Find It: Show the Topic Poster to the children. Say a word and ask several children to come to the front and find the picture on the poster. Then ask them to say the word on the list of words in the illustrated dictionary and read them aloud.

 Talk About...: Show the poster to the group. Ask the children questions about what they can see and get them to raise their hand to answer. For example, ask about colors (*Is it blue? / What color is it?*), about the position (*Where is the drum? / Is the boy next to the ocean?*), or numbers (*Are there three balloons? / How many triangles are there?*) and ask true or false questions (*It's a big ship / They don't have baseball bats*). Check that all the children are involved in the activity.

 Categories: Get the children to put the words of the Topic Poster into categories. Ask them to decide the nature of the categories and then take it in turns to say why they have grouped the words in this way. For example, *Lemonade and milk are drinks. / Salad and sausages start with 'S'.*

 Make a Picture Dictionary: During the school year, ask the children to make their own picture dictionary to take home with them. Ask them to cut out the words illustrated on the Black Line Masters and in the children's Activity Resource Book. They are to color the pictures and stick them on a blank sheet of paper, highlight them, and keep them in a folder. Encourage them to keep their personal illustrated dictionaries up to date and in a good condition.

 Cover Up: Show the Topic Poster for 20 seconds. Then cover part of the poster with your hand or with a colored sheet of paper. Ask the children to remember what was on the poster. After this, remove your hand or sheet of paper and cover something else on the poster.

 Echo: Show the Topic Poster. Get the children to look for words on the poster and repeat them aloud. After this, tell them that you are going to say some words. If the word is not on the poster, the children must remain silent. Encourage them to count to three before repeating the word, to make sure all the children say the word at the same time.

 Chain Game: Play a memory game with the words and concepts of the Topic Poster. Start the game by saying, *I can see (a/an + object) / (color)*. Ask one of the children to come to the front and point to the poster, repeating your sentence and then adding something else. Another child is to come to the front, point to another object or color, repeat the sentence and add something else. Continue in this way with other children.

 Name the Topic: Explain to the children that you are going to say words from some of the other Topic Posters they have studied. Brainstorm ideas about the topics the class has studied to establish the context. After this mention the key objects of the scenes and ask the children to name the topic, for example, *Pizza!* and the children should say *At the Restaurant!*

Big Book Builder Teacher's Notes

Vocabulary	Activities
Special Days birthday Christmas Day Easter Day Father's Day Halloween Mother's Day New Year's Eve Valentine's Day	**1 Dialogue development:** *Let's Celebrate!* track 47 Ask the children the name of a month when a special day is celebrated. Quickly review the months of the year and remind students how to pronounce them. Write the dialogue below on the board and underline the highlighted phrases, or write them in a different color. Ask students, as a group, to practice the dialogue line by line. Then divide the class into two and ask each team to take the part of A or B. Explain that the highlighted words can be replaced by others and ask the students to work in pairs to write their own dialogues, replacing the month and the special day. Ask pairs of children to come to the front and role play their dialogues. *A: What month is it?* *B: It's* **July***.* *A: Oh, good. It's* **my birthday** *this month.* *B: I love* **birthdays***!* *A: Me too!* **2 Riddle:** *Guess the Day!* Explain to the children that you are going to think about a special day. Tell the riddle then ask the children to name the special day, for example, *"It's Halloween!"* When the children have guessed all the dates, add other celebrations that are important in their culture. *I'm thinking of a special day,* *What can it be?* *It's in* **October***!* *You tell me!*
The Weather cloudy cold rainy snowy sunny windy coat pants shoes shorts sweater T-shirt	**1 Bounce Beat:** *Let's go out and play!* track 48 Copy the chant. Get the children to practice it line by line. Divide the class into six groups and give a type of weather to each group, including the word *windy*. Tell them that they will need to invent an action for each type of weather. Ask them to sing the chant while miming the action. *It's a* **windy** *day,* *It's a* **windy** *day,* *It's a* **windy** *day,* *Let's go out and play!* Explain to the children that they can change the type of weather in the chant after the first verse, invent their own verses and sing them using the same rhythm. **2 Class project:** *Class Weather Fashions* Children must work in groups and design clothes for the different seasons of the year in their country. They are to choose one type of weather and draw clothes for boys and girls suitable for that particular climate. Each group should come to the front of the class and show their designs and explain why they are suitable for a given season. Display the designs of the class to allow other groups in the school to see them. *A: "These clothes are for boys in summer; shorts, a T-shirt, sandals . . ."*

Vocabulary	Activities
3 Leisure Time color cry draw drink eat laugh paint play sing talk write	**1 Memory game:** *Picture Memory* Show the illustrated dictionary to students for 30 seconds and ask them to try to remember all the leisure time activities the people were doing. Close the Big Book Builder and ask children to work in groups and remember the 11 activities in the scene. Children are to write sentences such as: *A: A boy is playing with a hoop.* The group that finishes first and has remembered the activities correctly is the winner. **2 Spelling quiz:** *Action Words* Divide the class into two teams and draw a vertical line on the board. Say various action verbs ending in *-ing* and get children to come to the front and write them on the board. When you have finished saying all the words, the rest of the group has two minutes to make any corrections required. The teams will win one point for each word they have spelled correctly.

Vocabulary	Activities
4 **On Vacation** buy dance hold kiss make ocean sand sandcastle sleep swim	**1 Game:** *True or False* Tell the children that you are going to say sentences about the illustrated dictionary. Point to various parts of the scene and say a true or false sentence about the scene. If the sentence is true, the children are to stand up and repeat the sentence. If it is false, they must correct it: [point to the fish in the hammock]: *The fish are dancing.* *Ss: No, they aren't dancing! They're sleeping in hammocks.* Point to the seahorse that is singing. *The seahorse is singing.* *Ss: Yes! The seahorse is singing.* **2 Game:** *Miming* Ask the children to come to the front, one by one or in pairs or small groups. Whisper an action for them to mime. The rest of the class must say what they are doing.

Vocabulary	Activities
5 Numbers ten twenty thirty forty fifty sixty seventy eighty ninety one hundred	**1 Content activity:** *Number Grid* Ask the children to gather around you and show them Big Book Builder, Unit 5, *Numbers*. Explain the meaning of a number grid. Count all together from one to a hundred. Show them how to find the numbers on the grid moving your finger vertically along the multiples of tens and horizontally along the numbers from one to nine, in the upper section. Ask them to identify various objects and people on the pictures. *T: What is 33?* *Ss: Arm!* *T: What number is the green jello?* *Ss: Sixty-two!* **2 Game:** *Number Puzzle* Tell the children that you are going to dictate keys to help them find the numbers or pictures. Write them on the board: *cookie, yellow, water a plant, sandals, do homework, T-shirt.* Ask a few children to come to the front and identify the pictures on the number grid and point to the corresponding numbers. Write the numbers on the board below the corresponding pictures (for example, under *cookie*, write 53). If you think the children are capable of inventing their own riddles, ask them to write some and spend the rest of the class solving them. The children's riddles can be shorter than the above example.

Vocabulary	Activities
6 At the Hospital answer climb drive examine help operate on rescue take care of telephone	**1 Bounce Beat:** *He's Sick* *This little* **cat** *Is sick, sick sick!* *Take him to the hospital* *Quick, quick, quick!* Ask the children to point to the different animals on the poster and then invent their own verses. Ask more questions about the scene, for example, *What's the matter with the rabbit? Who can you see? etc.* **2 Game:** *Spot the Difference* Ask the children to look at the two pictures and spot any differences, for example, "*In picture A …. but in picture B…*" Write the example on the board. Tell them to look carefully at the picture and ask them to raise their hands and give more examples.

Vocabulary	Activities
7 At the Restaurant apple pie brownies fries hamburger jello lemonade milk pizza potato chips salad sausages soda	**1 Dialogue development:** *Eating Out* track 50 Tell the children that they are going to act out a dialogue in a restaurant. Ask them who works in a restaurant and ask them to say what sort of questions you ask to a waiter. At this point, it is acceptable that children answer in their own language. Write the first line of the dialogue of the waiter on the board and read it aloud. Ask the children to look at what the mother is eating and drinking (*salad, sausages, lemonade*), finish the dialogue on the board and ask the children to repeat the lines after you. Underline the highlighted words or write them in a different color, and explain that it is possible to change these words or the character for other people in the scenario. Ask the children to say what each member of the family is eating and then get them to form groups of five and act out the scene. Encourage the children to choose their own food and drinks! *Waiter: Can I take your order?* *Mom: Yes, please.* **Salad** *and* **sausages**, *please.* *Waiter: And to drink?* *Mom: A* **lemonade**, *please!* *Waiter: Coming up!* **2 Game:** *Draw and Guess* Tell the children that they are going to choose from a menu the food they like to eat in a restaurant. Show them the poster in the Big Book Builder, Unit 7, *At the Restaurant*. Ask them to draw a picture showing what they like to eat and drink. Tell them to walk around the room, but not to show their pictures. With a partner, they must try and guess what the other likes to order.

Vocabulary	Activities
8 The Concert band design poster practice prepare ears eyebrows eyes hair mouth nose teeth	**1 Game:** *Be the Teacher!* Ask students to think about the questions they could ask about the poster in the Big Book Builder; then write them on the board: *What is he / she doing?* *What are they doing?* *How many . . . are . . . -ing?* *Is he/she . . . -ing?* *Are they . . . -ing?* Ask a few children to come to the front to act as the teacher. They must point to the topic poster and ask questions about the people in the picture. Ask students to raise their hands before answering. Encourage the children to think about their own questions about the poster. **2 Bounce Beat:** *The School Show* **track 51** Play the chant and get students to listen to the entire track. Then get them to repeat each of the chant's verses until they can sing along with the track. Encourage the children to look at the picture and invent their own verses based on what the children are doing in the picture. *Playing music,* *Way to go!* *Making posters* *For the show!* *Singing songs,* *Way to go!* *Making costumes* *For the show!*

Vocabulary	Activities

Vocabulary

9 The Time

do the chores
early
get up
go to bed
have breakfast
have dinner
have lunch
late
read a story
recess

Activities

1 Dialogue development: *The Time*

track 52

Ask the children what time they do the various activities shown on the poster from the Big Book Builder. Get them to practice telling the time and point to 9:00. Ask *What time is it?* Ask the children to ask and answer questions about the activities they do and say the time when they do the activity in question. Practice with several times and activities.

A: *What time is it?*
B: *It's **9 o'clock***. *It's time **to go to bed** / **for bed***.

2 Game: *Charades*

Tell the children that you are going to say different times of day. Get them to mime an activity people do at that time.
Choose a few students and ask them what they are doing.

T: *What are you doing?*
Ss: *I'm having lunch.*

Then, ask the group what other children are doing:

T: *What's Anna doing?*
Ss: *She's doing homework.*

Scope and Sequence

	Grammar	Vocabulary	Subject Link
unit 1 Page 4	The first apartment is red. Which is the fourth month? When's Halloween? It's in October.	January, February, March, April, May, June, July, August, September, October, November, December, birthday, Mother's Day, Father's Day, Christmas, Valentine's Day, Halloween, Independence Day, Easter	Social Studies
unit 2 Page 12	What's he / she wearing? He's / She's wearing a sweater. What are you wearing? I'm wearing a red T-shirt. He / She isn't wearing shorts.	shorts, T-shirt, pants, sweater, shoes, coat, dress, sandals, sunny, windy, rainy, cloudy, snowy, cold	Math
unit 3 Page 20	What's he / she doing? He's / She's playing. He / She isn't measuring.	play, skate, sing, laugh, talk, eat, drink, cry, write, draw, color, paint, count, measure, paste, cut	Art
unit 4 Page 28	They're making sandcastles. What are they doing? They're buying ice cream cones. They aren't eating fish.	swim, buy, ice cream cone, sleep, make, sand, sandcastle, ocean, hold, dance, kiss, feed, trumpet, trainer, seal, rope	Social Studies
unit 5 Page 36	I'm calling my friends. I'm not cleaning my room. How many crayons does he have?	do homework, watch television, clean your room, call a friend, listen to music, water a plant, make a snack, ride a bicycle, numbers: twenty – one hundred	Math

Competency Icon Key

me

Activities that promote self-awareness

think

Activities that develop critical thinking skills

learn

Activities that promote the use of learning strategies

collaborate communicate

Activities that encourage cooperative work and effective communication

act

Activities that create global and social awareness

	Grammar	**Vocabulary**	**Subject Link**
 **unit 6** Page 44	Is he climbing through the window? Yes, he is. / No, he isn't. Is he rescuing a bird or a fish? He's rescuing a bird.	carry, take, run after, umbrella, climb, telephone, fruit, bag, rescue, help, take care of, fix, examine, drive, answer, operate on	Language
unit 7 Page 52	Are they eating apple pie? Yes, they are. / No, they aren't. Are the girls eating hamburgers or pizza?	pizza, hamburger, milk, lemonade, French fries, jello, salad, apple pie, set the table, wash the dishes, pour the drinks, serve the food, brownies, potato chips, soda, sausages	Natural Science
unit 8 Page 60	Are you designing the posters? Yes, I am. / No, I'm not. Are you coloring the eyes? Yes, we are. / No, we aren't.	poster, invitation, band, prepare, decorations, practice, design, decorate, eyes, ears, mouth, nose, eyebrows, teeth, hair, cheeks	Civics
unit 9 Page 68	What time is it? It's 2 o'clock. It's noon. Wilomena is playing with her friends. It's time for lunch. It's time to go to bed.	in the morning, in the afternoon, in the evening, at night, at noon, early, late, at midnight, have breakfast, have lunch, have dinner, get up, do the chores, recess, read a story, go to bed	Language

unit **1** LESSON **1**

 1 Listen and point. Say the words.
Track 2

January, February

January
February

March, April

March
April

May, June

May
June

July, August

July
August

September, October

September
October

November, December

November
December

2 Write the words in exercise 1.

unit 1

Lesson 1

Vocabulary presentation

Materials: track 02, colored pencils, Activity Resource Book page 5, Big Book Builder 2 pages 4 and 5

Lesson objectives: Learn the months of the year

New vocabulary: *January, February, March, April, May, June, July, August, September, October, November, December*

Global assessment indicators

a Student works well in teams
b Student presents work with care
c Student respects classroom rules
d Student is interested in learning

1 Bounce into action!

- Discuss with students how important and fun it is to learn another language.
- Remind them that with *Bounce Now* they will learn through games, songs and entertaining exercises.
- Tell students how you expect them to behave during the course.

2 Exercise 1

Listen and point. Say the words.

- Point to the pictures showing the months of the year and say *Listen and point.*
- Play track 02 and encourage students to point to the pictures.
- Point to your mouth and say *Say the words.* Play the track again and press the pause button after the name of each month so students can repeat them.

3 Exercise 2

Write the words in exercise 1.

- Ask students to write down the words.
- Go around the room helping and encouraging the students to say the words while they are writing them.

Optional Activity:

Big Book Builder 2 pages 4 and 5, *Special Days.* Do the activities suggested on pages xi to xix of this book.

4 Word window (optional activity)

- Ask students to open their Activity Resource Book to page 5.
- Ask them to write down the months in a chronological order in the boxes. Go around the room helping them.
- Ask them to draw a picture to represent each month. Encourage them to color them in.
- Divide the class into pairs. Ask them to show their calendar to their partner and say the months.

5 Bounce on!

1 Tell students that they are going to play a game to guess the months of the year in pairs. Pretend to be cold and elicit from them the months of *January* and *February*. Do the same thing with another couple of months. When a student guesses the pair of months correctly, they should come to the front and mime two more months for the others to guess. (5 – 10 minutes)

2 Write the months in any order on the board. Divide the class into groups and ask them to work in teams putting the months in the correct order. Then have a few of the groups come to the front to say the months in the correct order. The rest of the class is to correct them if they make any mistakes. (10 minutes)

Multi-ROM task   Student's Multi-ROM

Ask students to complete the Unit 1 Lesson 1 activity on the Student's Multi-ROM to review the vocabulary they have learned.

Interactive presentation. Use the Teacher's Multi-ROM to work with the Student's Book or with the Big Book Builder.

unit 1

Lesson 2

Grammar presentation

Materials: track 03, colored pencils

Lesson objectives:	Identify objects and their color in sequence
Vocabulary review:	Months of the year
New grammar:	*The first apartment is red.*

① Bounce into action!

- Write on the board six months of the year in any order. Ask students to memorize them.
- Tell the students to close their eyes. Erase one of the months. Ask them to identify the missing month. When students have understood how the game works, ask one of them to come to the front to take your place. Continue the game until all of the months have been reviewed.

② Exercise 1

 track 03

Listen and help Becky Bounce color the apartments.

- Write the ordinal numbers on the board. Ask students to stand and explain that they are going to go up a staircase with extremely big steps. Pretend to go up the staircase and say *First step.* Go up the next step and say *Second step.* Continue in this way until you reach the twelfth step.
- Repeat the action of going up the stairs and this time point to the numbers on the board.
- Explain to students that the apartments are colored differently for each floor. Play track 03 and ask them to point to the apartments in their books.
- Play the track again and stop it after each sentence so students can color in the apartment.
- Write *Today's grammar* on the board and ask students to copy it down.

Today's grammar

The	first / seventh	apartment is	red. / blue.

③ Exercise 2

Write sentences about the apartments.

- Point to the first apartment and ask *What color is the first apartment?* Help students answer *The first apartment is red.* Ask them to repeat the answer together and then individually.
- Continue in this way with the second and third apartments. Then ask students to complete the exercise on their own.

④ Bounce on!

1 On one side of the board, write the ordinal numbers (first, second, etc.). On the other, write the numbers in a different order (3rd, 2nd, etc.). Get several students to come to the front to match the words with the corresponding numbers. (5 – 10 minutes)

2 Divide the class into pairs. Tell them to ask and answer questions about the apartments in the book. *What color is the fifth apartment? The fifth apartment is purple.* Go around helping the pairs with their pronunciation. (5 – 10 minutes)

Home Study
page 77

Write the following task instruction on the board and ask students to copy it in the space provided:

"Match the words to the numbers."

 T5

Interactive presentation. Use the Teacher's Multi-ROM to work with the Student's Book or with the Big Book Builder.

Listen and help Becky Bounce color the apartments.

Track 3

Today's grammar

The first apartment is red.

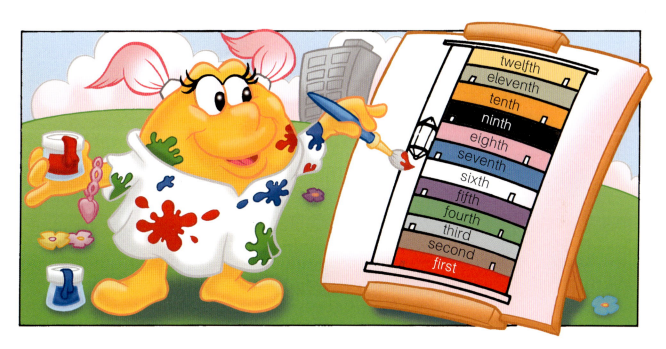

2 Write sentences about the apartments.

1 The first apartment is red .

5 The seventh apartment is blue .

2 The second apartment is orange

6 The eighth apartment is pink .

3 The third apartment is gray .

7 The eleventh apartment is beige.

4 The fifth apartment is purple .

8 The twelfth apartment is yellow.

1 Read the sentences. Write them in the correct order.

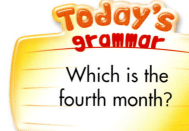
Today's grammar

Which is the fourth month?

The third month is March.

The eighth month is August.

The twelfth month is December.

The second month is February.

The ninth month is September.

The fifth month is May.

The first month is January.

The eleventh month is November.

The sixth month is June.

The tenth month is October.

The fourth month is April.

The seventh month is July.

1 The first month is January.

2 The second month is February.

3 The third month is March.

4 The fourth month is April.

5 The fifth month is May.

6 The sixth month is June.

7 The seventh month is July.

8 The eighth month is August.

9 The ninth month is September.

10 The tenth month is October.

11 The eleventh month is November.

12 The twelfth month is December.

2 Answer the questions.

1 Which is the fourth month?   April

2 Which is the eighth month?   August

3 Which is the twelfth month?   December

3 Write the questions.

1 Which is the second month ? February

2 Which is the first month ? January

3 Which is the eleventh month ? November

unit 1

Lesson 3

Grammar presentation

Materials: sheets of paper for each student

Lesson objectives:	Learn to ask about months in a chronological order
Vocabulary review:	Months of the year, ordinal numbers
New grammar:	*Which is the fourth month?*

1 Bounce into action!

- Check that students have completed and understood the task in the Home Study section, page 77. (Answers: p.166)
- Write the months of the year in a chronological order on the board and leave them there for the whole class.
- Count on your fingers and say *The first month is January*. Ask students to repeat the sentence.
- Then say *The second month is…* and wait for students to say *February*.
- Continue reviewing the ordinal numbers and the months in the same way.

2 Exercise 1

Read the sentences. Write them in the correct order.

- Read the sentences with the class.
- Get some of the students to come to the front and write the first sentences on the board.
- Ask students to complete the exercise on their own.

3 Exercise 2

Answer the questions.

- Do the correct mime and ask students *Which is the fourth month?* Help them to answer *April*.
- Repeat the same steps with the eighth and twelfth month. Then ask students to write down the answers in their books.
- Write *Today's grammar* on the board and ask students to copy it down.

Today's grammar		
Which is	the fourth	month?
	the eighth	

4 Exercise 3

Write the questions.

- Ask the class to read the list of months written on the board. Point to the word *April*; show four fingers and say *Ask me*. Help students to answer *Which is the fourth month?* Answer *April*.
- Repeat the same steps with the other months.
- Get students to write the questions in their books.

5 Bounce on!

1 Hand the sheets of paper to each student. Ask them to write their name and write the numbers from 1 to 12. Dictate the months of the year. Then ask the children to swap their sheets to check their answers. Write the number *1* on the board and ask a student to come to the front. Say *The first month of the year is January*. Ask the student to write the month and the rest of the class is to correct his/her spelling. Check that all the other students are doing it correctly. Continue in this way until completing all the months. (10 – 15 minutes)

2 Divide the class into teams. Write on the board *ninth month is the Which?* Ask them to put the question in the correct order and then answer it. One team member is then to write the question and answer on the board. If he/she writes it correctly, their team wins a point. The team with the most points is the winner. (10 minutes)

Interactive presentation. Use the Teacher's Multi-ROM to work with the Student's Book or with the Big Book Builder.

unit 1

Lesson 4

Song presentation

Materials: track 04, Activity Resource Book page 22, sheets of paper for each student, colored pencils

Lesson objectives: Learn the song *Months are fun to say!*
Review the months

Vocabulary review: Months of the year

 Bounce into action!

- Say the months of the year, two by two in chronological order, and ask students to mime the corresponding actions.
- Tell students they are going to say the months of the year in the reverse order, from December to January. Ask them to anticipate the months and mime the actions before you say the word.

 Exercise 1

 Sing the song: *Months are fun to say!*

- Explain to students they are going to listen to a song. Say *Listen* and play track 04.
- Play the track again and encourage students to say the months with the song.
- Model each line of the song and get students to repeat them all together.
- Play the track again and sing the song together.
- Ask students to open their Activity Resource Book to page 22 and do the activities.

 Exercise 2

Say the months in order. Then say them backwards.

- Ask students to say the months again in the correct order, but this time without help.
- Encourage them to say the months in the reverse order. Mime the actions, if you think it is necessary to help them.

 Exercise 3

Talk time. Say when your birthday is. Ask your friends.

- Tell students that your favorite month is October. Pretend to be emotional and say *My birthday is in October!*
- Ask them individually *When is your birthday?* Help them to answer.
- Tell the students that you are going to carry out a survey. Ask the students to write the months of the year on a piece of paper. Get them to go around the room asking their friends which is their birthday month, and to write the names next to the corresponding month.
- When they have finished, ask them to name the month when most students celebrate their birthday.

 Bounce on!

1 Divide the class into groups depending on where they are sitting. One student from each group is to say *My birthday is in….* and point to the next student and ask *When's your birthday?* The second student is to answer and then ask the same question to the next student. They are to continue in this way until all have answered and asked a question. When they have finished they should try to remember and name the months when the members of the group celebrate their birthdays. (5 – 10 minutes)

2 Hand a sheet of paper to each student. Ask them to write their name on the sheet and the sentence *My birthday is in (October)*. Then ask them to draw a picture. Display the pictures on the classroom walls to remember the dates of the students' birthdays. When it is someone's birthday, teach your students to sing *Happy Birthday!* (10 minutes)

Home Study
page 78

Write the following task instructions on the board and ask students to copy them in the space provided:

"Read and write the birthday months. Complete the sentence."

Multi-ROM task Student's Multi-ROM

Ask the students to listen to the song *Months are fun to say!*, track 04, at home until they have memorized it.

Interactive presentation. Use the Teacher's Multi-ROM to work with the Student's Book or with the Big Book Builder.

Sing the song: Months are fun to say!

Track 4

January, February, hip, hip, hooray!
January, February, months are fun
  to say!
March, April, we're singing our song!
March, April, come and sing along!

Hip, hip, hooray!

May, June, we're halfway through,
May, June, sing them too!
July, August, they're so much fun!
July, August, fun for everyone!

Hip, hip, hooray!

September, October, stamp your feet!
September, October, now keep
  that beat!
November, December, hip, hip, hooray!
November, December, months
  are fun to say!

Hip, hip, hooray!

2 Say the months in order. Then say them backwards.

January,
February, …

December,
November, …

Talk time

My birthday is in May.
When's your
birthday?

3 Say when your birthday is.
Ask your friends.

1 Listen and point. Say the words.

Track 5

birthday	Mother's Day	Father's Day	Christmas

Valentine's Day	Halloween	Independence Day	Easter

2 Complete the puzzle.

b i r t h d a y

M o t h e r ' s D a y

H a l l o w e e n

C h r i s t m a s

I n d e p e n d e n c e D a y

E a s t e r

F a t h e r ' s D a y

V a l e n t i n e ' s D a y

unit
1

Lesson 5
Vocabulary presentation

Materials: tracks 04 and 05, Big Book Builder 2 pages 4 and 5

Lesson objectives:	Learn about celebrations and festivals
New vocabulary:	birthday, Mother's Day, Father's Day, Christmas, Valentine's Day, Halloween, Independence Day, Easter

1 Bounce into action!

- Check that students have completed and understood the task in the Home Study section on page 78. (Answers: p.166)
- Play track 04 and sing the song *Months are fun to say!*
- Encourage them to mime the actions as they are singing. Play the track again if necessary.

2 Exercise 1

Listen and point. Say the words.

- Ask students to name any celebrations or festivals they know. Write their suggestions on the board, for example, *birthday*.
- Point to the pictures in the book and say all the words.
- Say *Listen and point* and play track 05. Get the students to point to the pictures as they hear them.
- Explain that the word *birthday* is not a proper noun and therefore is not written with a capital letter.
- Say *Say the words*, and play the track again. Press the pause button after each word to allow students to say them together.

3 Exercise 2

Complete the puzzle.

- Explain to the students that they are to complete the puzzle with the names of celebrations. Point to the picture of the cake and ask them to say what word it represents. Get one of the students to come to the front and write the word *birthday* on the board.
- Ask students to complete the rest of the crossword on their own.
- Go around the room helping and encouraging them to say the words while they are writing them down.

> **Optional Activity:**
> **Big Book Builder 2** pages 4 and 5, *Special Days*. Do the activities suggested on pages xi to xix of this book.

4 Bounce on!

1 Ask one of the students to come to the front and write the month you tell him/her. Then ask another student to write on the board a celebration held during that month. Correct any spelling mistakes and repeat the activity with other months. (5 – 10 minutes)

2 Erase the board, leaving only the names of the celebrations. Ask students to memorize the words and then to close their eyes. Erase one of the celebrations and ask students to open their eyes again. They must try to guess the missing word. Get one student to come to the front to write the missing word. Repeat the same steps with the other celebrations. (5 – 10 minutes)

Multi-ROM task   Student's Multi-ROM

Ask students to complete the Unit 1 Lesson 5 activity on the Student's Multi-ROM to review the vocabulary they have learned.

Interactive presentation. Use the Teacher's Multi-ROM to work with the Student's Book or with the Big Book Builder.

Lesson 6

Grammar presentation

Materials: drawings of special days, Big Book Builder 2 pages 4 and 5

Lesson objectives:	Learn to ask and answer questions about the months when special days are celebrated
Vocabulary review:	Special days, months of the year
New grammar:	*When's Halloween? It's in October.*

 Bounce into action!

- Write the special days on the board.
- Ask students to memorize the words and then to close their eyes. Erase one of the special days and ask students to open their eyes. They must guess which special day is missing.
- Get one of the students to come to the front to write the missing word on the board. Do the same thing with all the special days.

 Exercise 1

Write the special days in the correct month.

- Explain that you are going to name the special day and ask students to answer the name of the month when they are celebrated. Say *Christmas* and students are to answer *December*.
- After this, say the months of the year and get students to say the corresponding special day.
- Write *Halloween* on the board and ask *When's Halloween?* Help the students answer *In October*.
- Continue asking questions about the special days. Get students to answer all together and individually.
- Ask the students to open their books and write down the special days in the correct month.

 Exercise 2

Write sentences about six special days.

- Explain to students that they are going to write sentences about the month during which each special day is celebrated. Point to the word *Halloween* and ask again

When's Halloween? The students must answer *It's in October*. Model the structure *Halloween is in October* and write it on the board.

- Get several students to come to the front to write the following sentences on the board then ask the class to write the sentences in their books.

Today's grammar

When is	Christmas?	It's in	December.
	Halloween?		October.

Optional Activity:
Big Book Builder 2 pages 4 and 5, *Special Days*. Do the activities suggested on pages xi to xix of this book.

Bounce on!

1 Place pictures on the board representing the special days. Ask students to say the names when you point to them. Ask them to memorize them. Tell them to close their eyes. Remove one of the pictures and change the order. Ask the students to open their eyes and say the missing special day. Repeat the same steps with all the special days. (5 – 10 minutes)

2 Divide the class into two teams. Say a month and a special day to each team and get several students to come to the front and write the corresponding sentence. Say *December*, and the student is to write *Christmas is in December*. All students writing a correct sentence will win a point for their team. The team with the most points is the winner. (10 – 15 minutes)

 Home Study page 79

Write the following task instructions on the board and ask students to copy them in the space provided:

"Place the letters in the correct order to make words. Match the words to the picture. Choose a special day and draw a picture of it on the card and complete the sentence."

Interactive presentation. Use the Teacher's Multi-ROM to work with the Student's Book or with the Big Book Builder.

1 Write the special days in the correct month.

December
Christmas

November

January

August

May

June

March

February

October

September

Valentine's Day

Halloween

July

April

Becky Bounce's birthday

2 Write sentences about six special days.

1 Halloween is in October .

2 (students' own answers) .

3 (students' own answers) .

4 (students' own answers) .

5 (students' own answers) .

6 (students' own answers) .

 **you.**

1 Read Becky Bounce's answers to the questionnaire.

	Questions	Answers
1	What's your name?	Becky Bounce.
2	When's your birthday?	In July.
3	When's your mother's birthday?	In March.
4	When's your father's birthday?	In September.
5	Which is your favorite month?	December.
6	Why?	I like Christmas.

2 Complete the questionnaire about you and your family.

	Questions	Answers
1	What's your name?	(students' own answers)
2	When's your birthday?	(students' own answers)
3	When's your mother's birthday?	(students' own answers)
4	When's your father's birthday?	(students' own answers)
5	Which is your favorite month?	(students' own answers)
6	Why?	(students' own answers)

3 Write about you.

My name's __(own answers)__. My birthday is __(own answers)__.

My mother's birthday is __(students' own answers)__.

My father's birthday is __(students' own answers)__.

My favorite month is __(own answers)__ because __(own answers)__

_____.

unit 1

Write about . . . you.

Materials: track 04, a sheet of paper for each student, colored pencils, Big Book Builder 2 pages 4 and 5

Lesson objectives:	Read and ask questions about you
	Write a paragraph about you
Vocabulary review:	Months of the year, special days

① Bounce into action!

- Check that students have completed and understood the task in the Home Study section on page 79. (Answers: p. 166)
- Play track 04 and sing the song *Months are fun to say!* Divide the class into six groups, one group for two months. Each group is to sing two lines of the song.
- Point to the groups in the correct order and sing the song.
- Point to the groups randomly and sing the song in any order.

② Exercise 1

Read Becky Bounce's answers to the questionnaire.

- Ask students to open their books and read the questionnaire.
- Divide the class in two.
- Encourage one half to read the questions and the other to read the answers.

③ Exercise 2

Complete the questionnaire about you and your family.

- Ask students to answer the questionnaire individually.
- Go around the room helping and checking the students' work.

④ Exercise 3

Write about you.

- Explain to the students that they are going to use the information from exercise 1 to write a paragraph about themselves. Write on the board *My name's …* and ask a student to come to the front. Continue in the same way with all the sentences in exercise 3.
- Tell students that they are now going to complete a paragraph about themselves in their books, using the model on the board.
- While the students are working, go around the room helping and encouraging them to say the sentences as they are writing them down.

> **Optional Activity:**
> **Big Book Builder 2** pages 4 and 5, *Special Days*. Do the activities suggested on pages xi to xix of this book.

⑤ Bounce on!

1 Give a sheet of paper to each student and ask them to copy the questionnaire. Divide the class into pairs. Each student is to interview his/her partner and write down the answers. Go around the room helping the pairs with their pronunciation and checking they are working properly. (10 minutes)

2 Ask students to draw their partner and use the information from the questionnaire to write a paragraph on him/her. Go around the room helping and encouraging them. (10 – 15 minutes)

Interactive presentation. Use the Teacher's Multi-ROM to work with the Student's Book or with the Big Book Builder.

Lesson 8

Bounce around: Social Studies

Materials: pictures of annual, monthly and weekly calendars, sheets of paper, colored pencils, Big Book Builder 2 pages 4 and 5, Assessment Pack pages 4, 5 and 24

Lesson objectives: Learn through social studies
Develop critical thinking and reasoning
Review the vocabulary learned during the unit
Vocabulary expansion

New vocabulary: *calendar, day, month, week*

Vocabulary review: Months of the year

1 Bounce into action!

- Start by drawing something on the board that represents one of the special days, for example, a Christmas tree. Only draw part of the tree and get the students to try to guess the corresponding day and name it. If they cannot guess it, draw a little more of the object. Get one of the students to come to the front and write the special day on the board.
- Continue in this way for all the special days and festivals.

2 Exercise 1

What type of calendar is it? Circle the correct option.

- Look at the pictures of various calendars. Ask the children to say what these pictures have in common and what are the differences. Explain that there are different types of calendar: annual, monthly and weekly. Talk about the possible use for each type of calendar. Then ask the students to look at the pictures in their book and circle the correct option.

3 Exercise 2

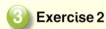

Choose two months. Draw why these months are special to you.

- Ask the students to name their favorite months and ask them why. Then ask students to choose two months of the year and in the corresponding space to draw the reasons why these months are important for them. Ask a few students to come to the front and talk about their pictures.

4 Exercise 3

Talk about the months.

- Ask the children to talk about their favorite and least favorite months. Go around the room encouraging and helping the pairs.

> **Optional Activity:**
> **Big Book Builder 2** pages 4 and 5, *Special Days.* Do the activities suggested on pages xi to xix of this book.

5 Bounce on!

1 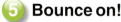 Divide the class into two teams. Invite one member of each team to come to the front. Say *Halloween* and they must write *October* on the board. The first child to write the word correctly wins a point for his/her team. The team with the most points in the winner. (10 minutes)

2 Write five months in any order on the board. Divide the class into pairs. Ask them to take turns asking and answering *Which is the third month? The third month is* (look at the corresponding month on the board). (5 – 10 minutes)

Language Assessment: Photocopy the language assessment sheet on page 24 of the Assessment Pack. Give each student a copy to complete in order to check what they have learned over the course of the unit.

 Self Assessment: Photocopy the self assessment sheet on page 4 of the Assessment Pack. Give a copy to each student for them to complete on their own. Offer help where necessary.

Global Assessment: Complete the global assessment on page 5 of the Assessment Pack. Check whether the objectives set out at the start of the unit were achieved by your students. Keep a record to refer back to in coming units.

 around: Social Studies

1 What type of calendar is it? Circle the correct option.

month (circled)
week
day

month
week (circled)
day

month
week
day (circled)

2 Choose two months. Draw why these months are special to you.

(students' own answers)

(students' own answers)

3 Talk about the months.

My birthday is in March.

Talk about

unit **2** LESSON **1**

 1 Listen and point. Say the words.
Track 6

shorts

shorts

T-shirt

T-shirt

pants

pants

shoes

shoes

coat

coat

sweater

sweater

sandals

sandals

dress

dress

2 Write the words in exercise 1.

unit 2

Lesson 1

Vocabulary presentation

Materials: track 06, pictures of clothing and footwear (on cards), Activity Resource Book page 7, empty boxes, paperclips, scissors, thread (optional), Big Book Builder 2 pages 6 and 7

Lesson objectives:	Learn vocabulary for clothing and footwear
New vocabulary:	*shorts, T-shirt, pants, sweater, dress, shoes, coat, sandals*

Global assessment indicators

a Student works well in teams
b Student presents work with care
c Student respects classroom rules
d Student is interested in learning

1 Bounce into action!

- Say the months of the year (two by two) in a chronological order and get students to do the appropriate mimes.
- Tell them that they are going to say the months in reverse order. Ask them to anticipate the months and mime the actions before you say the word.

2 Exercise 1

Listen and point. Say the words.

- On the board, draw the outline of a girl and a boy. Place one of the pictures of clothing on the outline and say the word.
- Ask several students to come to the front to place different types of clothing on the figures. Continue saying the clothing words as the students choose the various items.
- Point to the pictures in the book and say *Listen and point*.
- Play track 06 and have the students point to the clothing and footwear.
- Say *Say the words*. Play the track again and stop it after each word so students can repeat the word all together.

3 Exercise 2

Write the words in exercise 1.

- Ask students to write down the words.
- Go around the room helping and encouraging the students.

> **Optional Activity:**
>
> **Big Book Builder 2** pages 6 and 7, *The Weather*. Do the activities suggested on pages xi to xix of this book.

4 Word window (optional activity)

- Ask students to open their Activity Resource Book to page 7. Ask them to color in and cut out the pictures of clothing and footwear.
- Take a shoebox and place it on one side. Show them how to suspend a thread from one side of the box to the other to make a *wardrobe*.
- Divide the class into pairs. Students should show their cut-out clothing and shoes to their partner, saying the names and placing each item in the wardrobe with a paperclip.

5 Bounce on!

1 Divide the class into pairs. Students are to take turns pointing to the clothes his/her partner is wearing and say the words and color. (5 – 10 minutes)

2 Divide the class into two teams. Divide the board into two sections. Say the name of an item of clothing. One member from each team must come to the board, draw the item and write the name. Each correct answer will be awarded one point. (5 – 10 minutes)

Multi-ROM task   Student's Multi-ROM

Ask students to complete the Unit 2 Lesson 1 activity on the Student's Multi-ROM to review the vocabulary they have learned.

Interactive presentation. Use the Teacher's Multi-ROM to work with the Student's Book or with the Big Book Builder.

Lesson 2

Grammar presentation

Materials: track 07, photos and drawings of clothes and shoes

Lesson objectives: Learn to ask and answer questions about clothes and shoes

Vocabulary review: Clothes and shoes

New grammar: *What's he / she wearing? He's / She's wearing . . .*

❶ Bounce into action!

- Place the pictures and photos of clothes and shoes on the board.
- Ask students to say the words together as a group. When you are sure they remember the words, ask them to close their eyes. Remove one of the pictures and change the order of the words on the board.
- Ask the students to open their eyes and to tell you the missing picture. Continue in this way until you have practiced all the words.

❷ Exercise 1

track 07

Listen and number.

- Ask students to look at the picture. Point to Tom and say *What's he wearing?* Model the answer and get students to say it as a group (*He's wearing shorts*).
- Continue presenting the new structure in the same way.
- Write *Today's grammar* on the board and ask students to copy it down.

> **Today's grammar**
>
> What's he / she wearing?
>
> He's / She's wearing a sweater.

- Play track 07 and encourage students to point to the corresponding pictures.
- Play the track again and ask them to number the models.

Audioscript:

Benny Bounce: Welcome to the children's fashion show. And here is the first model. He's Tom. Tom's wearing green shorts and a yellow T-shirt. He's wearing brown sandals. And the second model is Samantha. Samantha's wearing a pink and purple dress. She's wearing white shoes.

Becky Bounce: The third model is Jason. What's Jason wearing? He's wearing black pants and a red sweater. Melinda's the fourth model. What's Melinda wearing? She's wearing a blue dress with a blue and green coat. Let's give our four models a big hand.

❸ Exercise 2

Answer the questions.

- Ask one of the students to read the first question for the whole class. Ask the other students to answer together *He is wearing green shorts, a T-shirt and sandals.*
- Have another student come to the front and write the answer.
- Ask them to complete the exercise on their own.

❹ Bounce on!

1 Divide the class into pairs. Each pair is to write the sentences about what they are wearing using the new grammar structure. Check the sentences and correct the spelling. Then get the students to form questions for each of the sentences they have written and ask them to each other. (10 minutes)

2 Divide the class into two teams. Ask a member from each team to come to the front. Say *Dress* and the children are to write the correct word on the board. The student writing the correct word first will be awarded one point. (5 – 10 minutes)

Home Study page 80

Write the following task instructions on the board and ask students to copy them in the space provided:

"Color the picture of Denzel Dog. Answer the question."

Interactive presentation. Use the Teacher's Multi-ROM to work with the Student's Book or with the Big Book Builder.

 Listen and number.

Today's grammar
What's he / she wearing?
He's / She's wearing a sweater.

2 Answer the questions.

1 What's Tom wearing?

He's wearing ___green shorts___, ___a yellow T-shirt___

and ___brown sandals___.

2 What's Samantha wearing?

___She's wearing a pink and purple dress and white shoes___.

3 What's Jason wearing?

___He's wearing black pants and a red sweater___.

4 What's Melinda wearing?

___She's wearing a blue dress and a blue and green coat___.

 **clothes.**

1 Write the questions.

1 <u>What's Tara wearing</u>   ?

She's wearing a yellow dress.

2 <u>What's Julian wearing</u>   ?

He's wearing an orange T-shirt.

Tara   Julian

2 Write more sentences about Tara and Julian's clothes.

Tara **1** <u>She's wearing a purple coat</u>   .

      2 <u>She's wearing brown shoes</u>   .

Julian **1** <u>He's wearing brown shorts</u>   .

      2 <u>He's wearing white sandals</u>   .

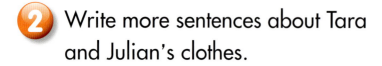

to Unit 1 Write the missing words.

First, second, third, <u>fourth</u>,
<u>fifth</u>, sixth, <u>seventh</u>,
eighth, <u>ninth</u>, <u>tenth</u>,
<u>eleventh</u>, twelfth.

unit 2

Lesson 3

Write about ... clothes.

Materials: sheet of paper for each student, colored pencils

Lesson objectives:	Ask and answer questions about clothes and shoes Write ordinal numbers
Vocabulary review:	Ordinal numbers, clothes and shoes
Grammar review:	*What's he / she wearing? He's / She's wearing . . .*

1 Bounce into action!

- Check that students have completed and understood the task in the Home Study section on page 80. (Answers: p.166)
- Get one of the students to come to the front and ask the class *What's he / she wearing?* and encourage them to answer *He's / She's wearing (a white T-shirt).* Repeat the same steps with several students.
- Have a student come to the front and divide the class into two. One team asks questions and the other answers them. Reverse the roles and continue in this way.

2 Exercise 1

Write the questions.

- Look at the illustrations of Tara and Julian with the students. Read the first answer together and ask them what is the first question (*What's she wearing?*). Ask them to repeat the question together and then invite a student to come to the front to write it on the board.
- Ask the students to read the answers and write the questions in their books.
- Go around the room helping them while they are working.

3 Exercise 2

Write more sentences about Tara and Julian's clothes.

- Ask students to look at the pictures of Tara and Julian and write sentences about what they are wearing.

4 Bounce back. Write the missing words.
(Review activity)

- Ask students to stand. Draw the picture of a simple staircase on the board and say *Let's go upstairs!* Pretend to go up the stairs and while you are doing this say *First step, second step, third step,* etc.
- Ask students to write the ordinal numbers in their books. Go around the room correcting their work.

5 Bounce on!

1 Hand a sheet of paper to each student. Ask them to draw a girl on one side and a boy on the other. Explain that you are going to describe the items of clothing and footwear each one is wearing and they have to draw them. Say *She's wearing green shorts. / He's wearing blue pants.* Give them enough time to draw and color them in. Continue in this way until they are fully clothed. (10 minutes)

2 Divide the class into pairs. Each pair is to give a name to the girl and boy on their sheet of paper and write sentences about them, such as, *Alicia's wearing green shorts and an orange T-shirt. She's wearing yellow sandals.* Have a few pairs come to the front to show their pictures and read their sentences. (10 minutes)

Interactive presentation. Use the Teacher's Multi-ROM to work with the Student's Book or with the Big Book Builder.

T14

unit 2

Lesson 4

Grammar and song presentation

Materials: track 08, colored pencils, Activity Resource Book page 23, various items of clothing, a box, Big Book Builder 2 pages 6 and 7

Lesson objectives:	Ask and answer questions about clothes they are wearing Sing the song *In my closet*
New grammar:	*What are you wearing? I'm wearing a red T-shirt.*

1 Bounce into action!

- Get several students to come to the front and ask them to draw pictures of clothing and then ask them to say the words all together and individually.
- Write the words on the board in any order and ask other students to come to the front and match up the word to the correct drawing.

2 Exercise 1

Draw a picture of you in your favorite clothes.

- Ask students to read the instruction together and encourage them to draw themselves wearing their favorite clothes.

3 Exercise 2

Answer the question.

- Ask a student to come to the front and ask him/her *What are you wearing?* Help the student to answer *I'm wearing a green sweater.* Ask them to repeat the question together.
- Ask the same question to different students.
- Write *Today's grammar* on the board and ask students to copy it down.

Today's grammar

What are you wearing?

I'm wearing a red T-shirt.

- Ask them to answer the question in their books.

4 Exercise 3

Talk time. Describe your clothes to your friends.

- Divide the class into pairs. Encourage them to ask and answer questions on the clothes they are wearing and the colors. *What are you wearing? / I'm wearing blue pants.*

5 Exercise 4

 Sing the song: *In my closet*

- Tell students that they are going to hear a song. Play track 08. Encourage students to hum the song as they are listening to it.
- Model each line of the song and get students to repeat the lines together.
- Play the track again and sing it together.
- Ask students to open the Activity Resource Book to page 23 and do the activities.

Optional Activity:

Big Book Builder 2 pages 6 and 7, *The Weather.* Do the activities suggested on pages xi to xix of this book.

---

6 Bounce on!

1 Write the lines of the song in any order on the board. Divide the class into groups and ask them to write the song correctly. When they have completed, play the track again so they can check their work. (10 minutes)

2 Place the clothing in the box. Ask one of the students to come to the front. Ask *What are you wearing?* And let them take one of the items of clothing out of the box. The student must describe and say the name of the garment they have taken. Repeat the activity by getting two other students to come to the front and ask one to ask the question and the other to take the item and answer the question. (10 minutes)

Home Study page 78
Write the following task instructions on the board and ask students to copy them in the space provided:
"Read the poem and draw a picture in the box. Write another verse for the poem."

Multi-ROM task Student's Multi-ROM
Ask the students to listen to the song *In my closet*, track 08, at home until they have learned it by heart.

Interactive presentation. Use the Teacher's Multi-ROM to work with the Student's Book or with the Big Book Builder.

1 Draw a picture of you in your favorite clothes.

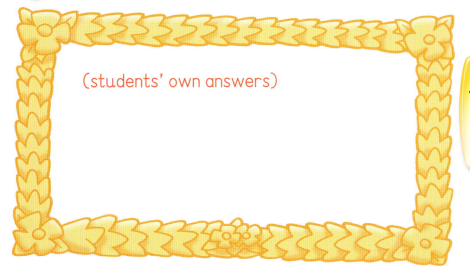

(students' own answers)

Today's grammar

What are you wearing?
I'm wearing a red T-shirt.

2 Answer the question.

What are you wearing?

I'm _(students' own answers)_

_____.

Talk time

I'm wearing blue pants.

3 Describe your clothes to your friends.

Track 8

Sing the song: In my closet

Shorts, shorts,
Yellow and blue,
In my closet,
And the T-shirts too!

In my closet!

Sweaters, sweaters,
Red and black,
On the shelf,
At the back!

In my closet!

Shoes, shoes,
To walk and run,
And my sandals,
For the sun!

In my closet!

 1 Listen and point. Say the words.
Track 9

sunny

windy

rainy

cloudy

snowy

cold

2 Describe the weather in each picture.

1 ___It's sunny___ .   **3** ___It's cloudy___ .   **5** ___It's rainy___ .

2 ___It's snowy___ .   **4** ___It's cold___ .   **6** ___It's windy___ .

16

Lesson 5

Vocabulary presentation

Materials: track 09, colored pencils, sheets of paper for each student, Big Book Builder 2 pages 6 and 7

Lesson objectives:	Learn vocabulary on weather
New vocabulary:	*sunny, windy, rainy, cloudy, snowy, cold*

1 Bounce into action!

- Check that students have completed and understood the task in the Home Study section on page 81. (Answers: p. 166)
- On the board, draw items representing different types of weather. Point to each picture and say the word.
- Repeat the words and encourage students to say them.
- Say the words and have a student come to the front and point to the corresponding elements.

2 Exercise 1

Listen and point. Say the words.

- Point to the pictures in the book and say *Listen and point.* Play track 09 and encourage students to point to the pictures.
- Play the track again and press the pause button after each word to allow students to say them all together.
- Point to the pictures on the board one by one and ask some of the students to repeat the words individually.

> **Optional Activity:**
>
> **Big Book Builder 2** pages 6 and 7, *The Weather.* Do the activities suggested on pages xi to xix of this book.

3 Exercise 2

Describe the weather in each picture.

- Look through the window, point to the weather and describe it by saying, for example, *It's (sunny).*
- Get students to repeat the sentence, first all together and then individually.
- Look at the pictures in the book and encourage students to identify the different types of weather.
- Ask them to write the sentences in their books. Go around the room helping and encouraging them.

4 Bounce on!

1 Hand a sheet to each student. Ask them to fold the sheet in two to form six boxes. In the first five boxes ask the students to write down the different types of weather learned during the lesson, and then draw the weather and the clothing most suitable for each type of weather. In the sixth box, ask the children to write their favorite weather and say why. (10 – 15 minutes)

2 Explain to students that they are going to say sentences about different types of weather. Ask students who have drawn a picture of a given type of weather to stand up and show their picture and sentence. Say *It's sunny/ It's cold* to practice. Continue in the same way with all types of weather. (5 – 10 minutes)

Multi-ROM task   Student's Multi-ROM

Ask students to complete the Unit 2 Lesson 5 activity on the Student's Multi-ROM to review the vocabulary they have learned.

Interactive presentation. Use the Teacher's Multi-ROM to work with the Student's Book or with the Big Book Builder.

unit 2

Lesson 6

Grammar presentation

Materials: track 08, Big Book Builder 2 pages 6 and 7

Lesson objectives:	Identify the clothes people are wearing
Vocabulary review:	Clothes, shoes and weather
New grammar:	*He / She isn't wearing shorts.*

1 Bounce into action!

- Sing the song *In my closet*. Play track 08 if students need help to remember the song.
- Divide the class into three groups, one for each verse of the song.
- Point to the groups randomly and encourage them to sing the verses in any order.

2 Exercise 1

Choose the correct clothes for the weather.
Put a ✓ or a ✗.

- Look at the pictures. Ask students to say what type clothes they would wear for each type of weather.
- Read the example all together and explain to the students that they need to put a ✓ or a ✗ in the correct box.

3 Exercise 2

Write the sentences. Complete the pictures.

- Have a student who is not wearing a coat to come to the front and say *He's / She's wearing a coat*. Ask the rest of the class to correct the sentence. Point to the student and say *He / She isn't wearing a coat*. Have students repeat the new structure together. Point to the student's clothes and encourage the others to say what they can see: *He's / She's wearing…*
- Get several students to come to the front and continue presenting the new structure in the same way.
- Write *Today's grammar* on the board and ask students to copy it down.

Today's grammar

| He / She isn't wearing | a coat. |
| | sandals. |

- Have students look at the pictures, and read the example sentence.
- Do the second example orally, and ask the students to write the answer.
- Go around the classroom offering help and encouragement.

Optional Activity:
Big Book Builder 2 pages 6 and 7, *The Weather*.
Do the activities suggested on pages xi to xix of this book.

4 Bounce on!

1 Divide the class into two teams. Draw the picture of a sun on the board and a boy in shorts and a T-shirt. Under the picture write the word *coat*. Students from both teams are to use the information on the board to write as many sentences as they can: *It's sunny, so he isn't wearing a coat. He's wearing shorts and a T-shirt.* The team writing the most correct sentences wins, as a point will be awarded for each sentence. (10 minutes)

2 Divide the class into teams. Write the following words on the board: *hot a wearing coat. It's she so isn't and sandals. wearing shorts She's* Ask them to put the sentence in the correct order. (*It's hot so she isn't wearing a coat. She's wearing shorts and sandals.*) (5 – 10 minutes)

Home Study
page 82

Write the following task instructions on the board and ask students to copy them in the space provided:

"Read and write the words under the pictures. Read about Mona Monster. Put a ✗ next to the clothes not used in exercise 1. Answer the question."

Interactive presentation. Use the Teacher's Multi-ROM to work with the Student's Book or with the Big Book Builder.

Choose the correct clothes for the weather. Put a ✓ or a ✗.

1  ✓   ✗

2  ✗   ✓

3  ✗   ✓

4  ✓   ✗

 Write the sentences. Complete the pictures.

1  It's ___snowy___ so she ___isn't wearing shorts___.
She's wearing a coat and a hat and shoes .

2  It's ___rainy___ so she ___(students' own answers)___.
_____.

3  It's ___windy___ so he ___(students' own answers)___.
_____.

4  It's ___sunny___ so he ___(students' own answers)___.
_____.

1 Listen and read. *My favorite clothes.*

Track 10

1

Damian: It's cloudy, Patsy! Don't wear those clothes to the park. Put your coat on!

Patsy: No! I'm wearing my shorts and my T-shirt! They're my favorite clothes!

2

Damian: Run, Patsy! It's cloudy and it's cold!

Patsy: No! I'm not wearing my sports shoes. I'm wearing my sandals!

Damian: Girls!

3

Damian: Look, Patsy! It's rainy now. And I have a coat!

4

Patsy: Look! I have a coat too. Isn't it neat? And black's my favorite color! Now don't talk anymore. Let's play!

2 Circle the clothes that aren't in the story.

coat   shoes   (dress)   shorts   (sweater)   T-shirt   (pants)   sandals

18

Lesson 7

Read a story

Materials: track 10, five photocopies of the story, Big Book Builder 2 pages 6 and 7

Lesson objectives: Consolidate the unit's language by reading a story
Vocabulary review: Clothes, shoes, weather

1 Bounce into action!

- Check that students have completed and understood the task in the Home Study section on page 82. (Answers: p.166)
- Explain to students that they are going to listen to a story.
- Look at the pictures and ask the students what sort of weather is mentioned and also ask what they think the story will be about.
- Write some of their suggestions on the board.

2 Exercise 1

Listen and read. *My favorite clothes.*

- Say *Listen* and play track 10. Encourage students to point to the pictures as they are mentioned in the story.
- Ask them to say what the story is about. Point to the suggestions on the board and check any similarities to the story they have just listened to.
- Talk about Patsy's actions.
- Play the track again and encourage students to read the story while they are listening to it.

3 Exercise 2

Circle the clothes that aren't in the story.

- Ask students to read the story on their own and circle the clothes that are not in the story.
- Go around the room helping them.

Optional Activity:

Big Book Builder 2 pages 6 and 7, *The Weather.* Do the activities suggested on pages xi to xix of this book.

4 Bounce on!

1 Read the story's dialogue and have students repeat the lines a few times together. Divide the class into pairs and ask them to practice the dialogue. Walk around helping the pairs with their pronunciation. Then ask a few of the pairs to act out the dialogue for the whole class. (10 minutes)

2 Photocopy the dialogue of the song and cut it into strips. Divide the class into five groups. Give each group the photocopies cut into strips and get them to put the story in the correct order. The first team that manages to put the story in the correct order is the winner. (10 – 15 minutes)

Multi-ROM task   Student's Multi-ROM

Ask the students to listen to the story *My favorite clothes*, track 10, at home until they have memorized it.

Interactive presentation. Use the Teacher's Multi-ROM to work with the Student's Book or with the Big Book Builder.

unit
2

Lesson 8

Bounce around: Math

Materials: pictures of various colored gloves, blank sheets of paper, colored pencils, Assessment Pack pages 4, 5 and 25

Lesson objectives:	Learn through mathematics
	Develop critical thinking and reasoning
	Review the vocabulary learned during the unit
	Vocabulary expansion
Vocabulary review:	Numbers
New vocabulary:	*fingers, gloves*

 Bounce into action!

- Ask students to come to the front and act out the story, *My favorite clothes*, in pairs.

 Exercise 1

 Read the questions. Circle the correct answer.

- Place the picture of a glove on the board. Say *glove* and ask students to repeat the word. Ask *How many fingers are there in a glove?* Count the fingers with them. Repeat the activity but change the number of gloves and ask the students to count the total number of fingers. Then ask the children to read the questions and circle the correct answers.

Exercise 2

Talk about your answers.

- Ask students to look at the answers and circle them in their books. Say *Let's talk about the answers.*
- Do the first question and ask the students to say the correct answer.

 Bounce on!

1 Hand out blank sheets of paper. Ask the children to draw their hands in order to make gloves. Ask them to color in the shapes and then cut them out. Then form small groups and get students to add and subtract the number of fingers. (5 – 10 minutes)

2 Divide the group into two teams. Ask a member from each team to come to the front and to say a sum, for example, four fingers plus three fingers. The children are to calculate the number of fingers and write the correct answer on the board. The first student to answer correctly wins a point for his/her team. Increase the difficulty by asking them to add larger numbers. (10 – 15 minutes)

Language Assessment: Photocopy the language assessment sheet on page 25 of the Assessment Pack. Give each student a copy to complete in order to check what they have learned over the course of the unit.

 Self Assessment: Photocopy the self assessment sheet on page 4 of the Assessment Pack. Give a copy to each student for them to complete on their own. Offer help where necessary.

Global Assessment: Complete the global assessment on page 5 of the Assessment Pack. Check whether the objectives set out at the start of the unit were achieved by your students. Keep a record to refer back to in coming units.

Interactive presentation. Use the Teacher's Multi-ROM to work with the Student's Book or with the Big Book Builder.

Bounce around: **Math**

① Read the questions.
Circle the correct answer.

a. How many fingers are there in a glove?   4   ⑤   6

b. How many fingers are there in 4 gloves?   10   15   ⑳

c. How many fingers are there in a pair of gloves?   ⑩   12   13

d. Look at Tom's gloves. How many fingers are there?   5   ⑩   15

e. How do you reach your answer in b?   5 + 5 + 5 + 5   4 x 5

② Talk about your answers.

There are 10 fingers
in 2 gloves.

There are 5 fingers
in 1 glove.

Talk
about

 1 Listen and point. Say the words.

Track 11

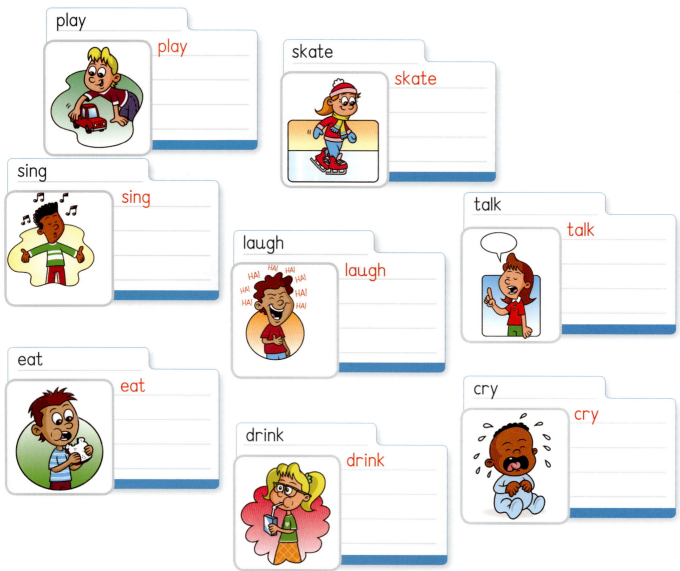

play

play

skate

skate

sing

sing

laugh

laugh

talk

talk

eat

eat

drink

drink

cry

cry

2 Write the words in exercise 1.

20

unit 3

Lesson 1

Vocabulary presentation

Materials: tracks 04 and 11, Activity Resource Book page 9, colored pencils, Big Book Builder 2 pages 8 and 9

Lesson objectives: Learn action verbs

New vocabulary: *play, skate, talk, sing, laugh, cry, eat, drink*

Global assessment indicators

a   Student works well in teams
b   Student presents work with care
c   Student respects classroom rules
d   Student is interested in learning

① Bounce into action!

- Sing the song *Months are fun to say!* Play track 04 to help students remember the song.

② Exercise 1

Listen and point. Say the words.

- Point to each picture in the book; say the word and perform the appropriate action. Have students copy the action.
- Point to the sentences in the book and say *Listen and point*. Play track 11 and encourage students to point to the pictures.
- Say *Say the words*. Play the track again and stop it after each word so students can repeat the words, first as a group and then individually.

③ Exercise 2

Write the words in exercise 1.

- Ask students to write down the words.
- Go around the room helping and encouraging the students to say the words they are writing.

> **Optional Activity:**
> **Big Book Builder 2** pages 8 and 9, *Leisure Time*. Do the activities suggested on pages xi to xix of this book.

④ Word window (optional activity)

- Ask students to open their Activity Resource Book to page 9. Ask them to fold the page using the straight lines and cut it out along the dotted line. Have them write one of the verbs in each of the eight figures. Encourage them to decorate their chain.
- Divide the class into pairs. Each student should show their chain of figures to his/her partner and take turns saying the verbs. Encourage them to point to the figure, say the word and do the corresponding action.

⑤ Bounce on!

1 Write the verbs on the board. Give students enough time to memorize them and ask them to close their eyes. Erase one of the verbs. Ask them to open their eyes and say the missing verb. Continue in this way until they have identified all the verbs. (5 – 10 minutes)

2 Play *Bounce Says*. Explain to students that if you say the phrase *Bounce says*, they must perform the action; however, if you don't say *Bounce says*, they must remain still. Say *Bounce says cry*, and they must pretend to cry. Say *Play!* and the students are to remain motionless. Students doing the wrong action or moving when they should not are out of the game. (5 – 10 minutes)

Multi-ROM task   Student's Multi-ROM

Ask students to complete the Unit 3 Lesson 1 activity on the Student's Multi-ROM to review the vocabulary they have learned.

Interactive presentation. Use the Teacher's Multi-ROM to work with the Student's Book or with the Big Book Builder.

T20

Lesson 2

Grammar presentation

Materials: track 12, colored pencils, blank sheets of paper

Lesson objectives:	Learn to ask and answer questions about action verbs
Vocabulary review:	*play, skate, talk, sing, laugh, cry, eat, drink*
New grammar:	*What's he / she doing? He's / She's playing.*

① Bounce into action!

- Mime one of the actions and elicit the verb from students. Pretend to sing. Students are to say *Sing!* Ask one of the students to come to the front and write the word on the board. Continue in this way to practice all the verbs.
- Divide the class in half. Point to the verbs randomly and have half the students say the word while the other half mime the action.

② Exercise 1

Listen and number the pictures.

track 12

- Call one of the students to the front and whisper one of the verbs in his/her ear. Ask the student to mime the action. Ask the class *What's he/she doing?* Help them to answer *He's/She's laughing.* Have students repeat the new structure together.
- Repeat the same steps with all the verbs.
- Write *Today's grammar* on the board and ask students to copy it down.

Today's grammar

What's he / she doing?

He's / She's | skating.
laughing.
drinking.

- Play track 12 and ask students to number the pictures.

③ Exercise 2

Match the pictures with the sentences in exercise 1.

- Ask a few students to read the sentences for the whole class.
- Ask the class to draw a line from each sentence to the correct picture.

④ Bounce on!

1 Divide the class into pairs. Tell them to look at the pictures in their books and take turns asking and answering questions such as *What's he/she doing? He's /She's...* Go around helping the pairs with their pronunciation. (5 – 10 minutes)

2 Hand out blank sheets of paper. Dictate a few short sentences using the verbs learned during the lesson. Ask them to circle the verbs in each sentence and draw a picture of each one. (15 – 20 minutes)

Home Study
page 83

Write the following task instruction on the board and ask students to copy it in the space provided:

"Complete the words. Look at the pictures and write the sentences."

Interactive presentation. Use the Teacher's Multi-ROM to work with the Student's Book or with the Big Book Builder.

1 Listen and number the pictures.

Track 12

Today's grammar

What's he / she doing?
He's / She's playing.

6

8

He's playing.

She's skating.

7

1

He's talking.

She's laughing.

2

3

She's singing.

She's crying.

4

5

He's eating.

He's drinking.

2 Match the pictures with the sentences in exercise 1.

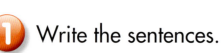 **1** Write the sentences.

1 She's _talking_.

4 She's laughing.

7 She's skating.

2 She's singing.

5 She's eating.

8 She's crying.

3 She's playing.

6 She's drinking.

Bounce back

to Unit 2 Answer the question.

What are you wearing today?

(students' own answers).

Lesson 3

Consolidation and review

Materials: Big Book Builder 2 pages 8 and 9

Lesson objectives:	Practice and consolidate the verbs learned Review language relating to clothes
Vocabulary review:	*play, skate, talk, sing, laugh, cry, eat, drink, clothes and footwear*
New grammar:	*He's / She's laughing.*

1 Bounce into action!

- Check that students have completed and understood the task in the Home Study section on page 83. (Answers: p.166)
- Have one of the students come to the front and whisper in his/her ear one of the verbs. They should mime the action. Ask the class *What's he/she doing?* The students must reply *He/She's talking*, for example.
- Repeat the same steps with the other verbs.

2 Exercise 1

Write the sentences.

- Look at the pictures with the students. Point to the first picture of the girl and ask *What's she doing?* Students are to answer *She's talking*. Have one of the students come to the front to write the sentence on the board.
- Repeat the same steps with the second picture. Ask them to write the sentences in their books.
- Go around the room helping and encouraging them.
- Ask a few of the students to read the sentences aloud and correct their work as a class.

3 Bounce back. Answer the question.
(Review activity)

- Ask several students *What are you wearing?* and have them describe the clothes and shoes they are wearing. They are to say the color of each garment, for example *I'm wearing a green T-shirt, gray pants and black shoes.*
- Ask students to answer the question in their books.
- Go around the room helping them and correcting the sentences.

Optional Activity:

Big Book Builder 2 pages 8 and 9, *Leisure Time*. Do the activities suggested on pages xi to xix of this book.

4 Bounce on!

1 Play *Hangman!* Divide the class into two teams. The students in one team are to think of a verb. Get one student from one of the teams to come to the front and draw a dash instead of each letter in the verb. The other team is to say a letter of the alphabet to guess the word. If the letter is in the word, the student at the front must write the letter in the word; if the letter is not in the word, he/she must draw part of the person being hanged (i.e. head, body and limbs). When the team guesses the word or the other team has finished drawing the hangman, the teams are to change places. (5 – 10 minutes)

2 Jumble up the letters of one of the verbs. Get one of the students to come to the front and write the correct verb below the scrambled up word. Then ask a few of the students to mime the corresponding action. Repeat the same steps with several different verbs. (5 – 10 minutes)

Interactive presentation. Use the Teacher's Multi-ROM to work with the Student's Book or with the Big Book Builder.

Consolidation

Materials: music, colored pencils, Big Book Builder 2 pages 8 and 9

Lesson objectives:	Consolidate the action vocabulary
Vocabulary review:	*play, skate, talk, sing, laugh, cry, eat, drink*
New grammar:	*What's he doing? He's . . .*

1 Bounce into action!

- Explain to students that while the music is playing you will say a word and they must walk about the room doing the appropriate action. When you stop the music they must stop moving. Any student doing the wrong action, or moving when they should remain motionless, is out of the game.
- Repeat the same procedure to practice all the verbs.

2 Exercise 1

Draw a picture of Marvin the Monster doing a different activity. Write sentences.

- Look at the pictures of Marvin the Monster. Ask them *What's he doing? (He's eating a hotdog).*
- Read the second sentence about Marvin.
- Ask students to suggest what Marvin could be doing on the other pages of the book.
- Ask them to draw a picture of Marvin doing a different activity.
- Go around the room admiring their pictures and encouraging them to say the corresponding sentences.

3 Exercise 2

Talk time. Tell your friends about Marvin the Monster.

- Divide the class into pairs. Each student is to show his/her pictures of Marvin to a partner and read out the sentences they have written.
- Go around helping the pairs with their pronunciation.

Optional Activity:

Big Book Builder 2 pages 8 and 9, *Leisure Time.* Do the activities suggested on pages xi to xix of this book.

4 Bounce on!

1 Play *Tic-tac-toe.* Write on the board *What's Marvin doing?* Below the sentence draw a 3-by-3 grid. Write a verb in each square. Divide the class into two groups: the *Os* and the *Xs.* Ask each group to choose a square and use the verb correctly in a sentence. For example, if they choose *cry,* they are to say *He's crying.* If they say the sentence correctly, they can place their mark (O or X) on the grid. The first team to have three marks in a row is the winner. (10 minutes)

2 Ask different students to come to the front and have them pretend to be Marvin. Whisper a verb to a student and encourage him/her to do the action. The rest of the class is to guess the action. The student who guesses correctly should come to the front and perform the next action. (5 – 10 minutes)

Home Study page 84

Write the following task instruction on the board and ask students to copy it in the space provided:

"Write a story about Toby Turtle. Use the words in the box."

Interactive presentation. Use the Teacher's Multi-ROM to work with the Student's Book or with the Big Book Builder.

 Draw a picture of Marvin the Monster doing a different activity. Write sentences.

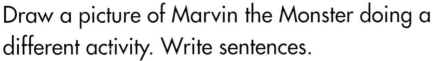

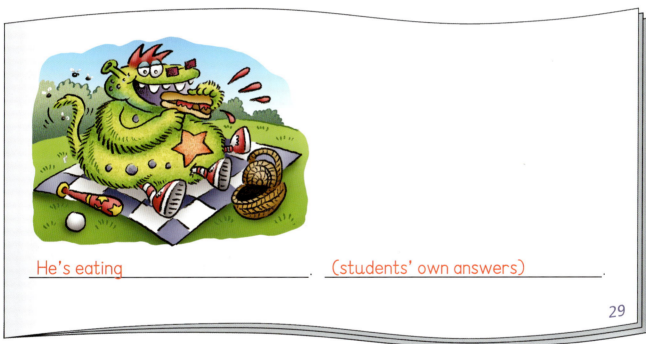

He's eating _____. (students' own answers) _____.

29

 Tell your friends about Marvin the Monster.

Talk time

Look, he's eating.

1 Listen and point. Say the words.

Track 13

write 	draw 
color 	paint 
count 	measure 
paste 	cut 

2 Complete the words. Match them to the pictures.

1 c _o_ l _o_ r

2 p _a_ _s_ _t_ e

3 d _r_ a _w_

4 c _o_ _u_ n t

5 m _e_ a _s_ _u_ r _e_

6 c _u_ t

7 w _r_ i _t_ e

8 p _a_ _i_ n _t_

24

Lesson 5

Vocabulary presentation

Materials: track 13, pens, pencils, crayons, scissors, paintbrush, ruler, glue, non-transparent bag

Lesson objectives:	Learn more action words
New vocabulary:	*write, draw, color, paint, count, measure, paste, cut*

1 Bounce into action!

- Check that students have completed and understood the task in the Home Study section on page 84. (Answers: p.166)
- Show a pencil and say *Write* and do the corresponding action. Have students do the same action.
- Show various objects in any order and ask students to say the words and mime the actions.
- Change the order and increase the speed at which you show the objects.

2 Exercise 1

Listen and point. Say the words.

- Point to the pictures in the book and say *Listen and point*. Play track 13 and encourage students to point to the pictures as they hear the actions on the track.
- Say *Say the words*. Play the track again and press the pause button after each word so students can repeat the words together.
- Point to the pictures on the board in any order and ask students to repeat the words individually.

3 Exercise 2

Complete the words. Match them to the pictures.

- Explain to students that they must complete the missing letters.
- Ask students to draw a line from each word to the corresponding picture.
- Go around the room helping and correcting their work.

4 Bounce on!

1 Divide the class into two teams. Ask one member from each team to come to the front. Spell out a verb and get them to write it on the board. The first student to write the word correctly will win a point for his/her team. (10 – 15 minutes)

2 Divide the class into two teams. Write the verbs on the board. Place the objects into a non-transparent bag. Have students come to the front, remove an object from the bag and say the appropriate verb. Students saying and erasing the word correctly will win a point for their team. (5 – 10 minutes)

Multi-ROM task   Student's Multi-ROM

Ask students to complete the Unit 3 Lesson 5 activity on the Student's Multi-ROM to review the vocabulary they have learned.

Interactive presentation. Use the Teacher's Multi-ROM to work with the Student's Book or with the Big Book Builder.

Lesson 6

Grammar and song presentation

Materials: track 14, colored pencils, Activity Resource Book page 24, Big Book Builder 2 pages 8 and 9

Lesson objectives:	Learn to use verbs in a negative form
	Sing the song *Old Mr. Lilly*
Vocabulary review:	*writing, drawing, coloring, painting, counting, measuring, pasting, cutting*
New grammar:	*He / She isn't counting.*

1 Bounce into action!

- Play *Bounce says* with the verbs. Say *Bounce says paint*, and students are to do the correct action. Say *Count!* and the students should remain still. Continue in the same way with the other verbs. Students doing the wrong action, or moving when they should not, are out of the game.

2 Exercise 1

Read the sentences. Put a ✓ or a ✗ next to the pictures.

- Get one of the students to come to the front and whisper to them that they should draw something on the board. Say to the class *Look! He's / She's counting.* Get students to correct the statement and say *No!* Point to the student and say *He / She isn't counting. He's / She's drawing.* Get students to repeat the sentences together several times. Present the other verbs in the same way.
- Write *Today's grammar* on the board and ask students to copy it down.

Today's grammar	
He / She isn't	painting counting.

- Read the sentences in the book with students.
- Ask them to look at the pictures and check (✓) the correct picture and place a (✗) next to the incorrect one.
- Go around the room helping them.

3 Exercise 2

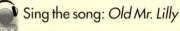

Sing the song: *Old Mr. Lilly*

- Tell students they are going to listen to a song. Play track 14 and mime the actions.
- Play the track again and encourage students to mime the actions.
- Model each line in the song and get students to repeat the lines together.
- Play the track again and sing the song together.
- Ask students to open their Activity Resource Book to page 24 and do the activities.

Optional Activity:

Big Book Builder 2 pages 8 and 9, *Leisure Time.* Do the activities suggested on pages xi to xix of this book.

4 Bounce on!

1 Divide the class into three teams, one for each verse of the song. Point to the groups in turn and sing the song. Then point to the groups randomly and sing the song in any order. (5 – 10 minutes)

2 Instruct the students to draw and color *Mrs. Lilly.* Say *Draw Old Mrs. Lilly. She isn't writing. She isn't measuring. She isn't counting. She's painting.* (10 minutes)

Multi-ROM task   Student's Multi-ROM

Ask the students to listen to the song *Old Mr. Lilly,* track 14, at home until they have memorized it.

Interactive presentation. Use the Teacher's Multi-ROM to work with the Student's Book or with the Big Book Builder.

1 Read the sentences. Put a ✓ or a ✗ next to the pictures.

 **Today's grammar** He / She isn't measuring.

1 He isn't measuring. He's painting. ✓ ✗

2 She's pasting. She isn't cutting. ✗ ✓

3 He's counting. He isn't coloring. ✓ ✗

4 She's writing. She isn't drawing. ✓ ✗

5 He isn't pasting. He's coloring. ✗ ✓

2  Track 14 **Sing the song: Old Mr. Lilly**

Look at old Mr. Lilly.
He's on his knees,
And he's looking silly.
What's he doing on the floor?
Let's get closer,
And find out more.

He isn't writing.
No, not now.
He isn't pasting.
No, no way!

Mr. Lilly's counting,
1, 2, 3.
He's measuring the space
For his new TV!

Write about

Rowena and Nutty.

1 Read about Rowena.

Rowena is at school. She isn't coloring. She isn't drawing. She's painting. It's a flower. It's pink and green. Look! Now she's pasting the flower in her book. What a beautiful flower! Rowena is very happy.

2 Write about Nutty.

Nutty is at school. He isn't ___painting___. He isn't ___coloring___. He's ___drawing___. It's a ___tree___. It's ___green___ and ___brown___. Look! Now ___he's pasting the tree___ in his book. What ___a beautiful tree___! Nutty ___is very happy___.

Lesson 7

Write about . . . Rowena and Nutty.

Materials: track 14, one sheet of paper for each student, colored pencils

Lesson objectives:	Read a text and answer questions Write a paragraph about Nutty
Vocabulary review:	*writing, drawing, coloring, painting, counting, measuring, pasting, cutting*
New grammar:	*She isn't drawing. She's painting.*

1 Bounce into action!

- Sing the song *Old Mr. Lilly*. Play track 14 to help them remember the song.
- Encourage students to perform the actions of the song.

2 Exercise 1

Read about Rowena.

- Read the paragraph about Rowena with the class.
- Ask some students to read the sentences aloud.
- Discuss the actions of Rowena. Ask questions to check their comprehension: *What's she doing? / What's she painting? / Where's she pasting the flower? / Is Rowena happy?*

3 Exercise 2

Write about Nutty.

- Look at the first picture of Nutty and say *Look, he's writing.* Encourage them to correct the statement and say *He isn't writing!* Point to the picture again and say *He's measuring.* Encourage them to say *He isn't measuring!* Ask them *What's he doing?* They should answer *He's drawing.*
- Continue asking questions about the pictures *What's he drawing? / What color is it? / What's he doing now?*
- Ask students to complete the paragraph about Nutty in their books.
- Go around the room helping and encouraging them.

4 Bounce on!

1 Divide the class into pairs (A and B). Hand a sheet of paper to each student and tell them to draw a picture of Henry, the hamster. Tell them that you are going to say different sentences for each pair (A and B) and they must listen and draw the correct sentence. Say *A: Henry is at school. He isn't counting. He isn't measuring. He's drawing an apple. B: Look! Now he's coloring the apple red. What a beautiful apple. Henry is very happy.* (10 – 15 minutes)

2 Each student should show their picture of Henry to his/her partner and say the actions. Go around helping the pairs with their pronunciation. (5 minutes)

Home Study page 85

Write the following task instructions on the board and ask students to copy them in the space provided:

"Read about how to make a butterfly. Circle is or isn't. Read the instructions and make a flower."

Interactive presentation. Use the Teacher's Multi-ROM to work with the Student's Book or with the Big Book Builder.

unit 3

Lesson 8
Bounce around: Art

Materials: cards, scissors, tape, colored pencils, Assessment Pack pages 4, 5 and 26

Lesson objectives: Learn through art
Review the vocabulary learned during the unit
Vocabulary expansion

Vocabulary review: *finger, verbs*

New vocabulary: *puppet*

1 Bounce into action!

- Check that students have completed and understood the task in the Home Study section on page 85. (Answers: p.166)
- Ask students to stand up next to their chairs. Say different actions and get students to do the corresponding mime. Say *Play* and they have to pretend to play.
- To retain the attention and interest of the students, change the order and speed at which you say the words.

2 Exercise 1

Make a finger puppet.

- Look at the materials all together and give the students what they need.
- Ask students to follow the instructions and get them to decorate their finger puppets.
- Divide the class into pairs. Each student should show their finger puppet to his/her partner. Ask them to take it in turns to ask and answer questions with their finger puppets.

3 Exercise 2

Talk about your finger puppet.

- Point to one of the students and say *What is* (name of their finger puppet) *doing?*
- Ask the student to answer using the full grammar structure *He / She is (laughing).*
- Then ask students to form pairs and continue asking and answering questions of each other.
- Go around the room checking they are doing the activity correctly.

4 Bounce on!

1 Place a puppet on your finger. Explain to students that you are going to say sentences about the puppet on your finger. Ask students to touch their nose with their finger if what you are saying is correct and to put up their hands and correct it if it is not true. Do a practice round. Pretend that your finger puppet is eating and say *He's eating*. Students must touch their nose. Then pretend your finger puppet is counting and say *He's painting*. Students must raise their hands and say *He isn't painting. He's counting.*
(5 – 10 minutes)

2 Divide the class into three or four teams. Give a pen and a card to each team. Tell them that they have five minutes to write five sentences about the actions they most like to do and that they can do with their finger puppets. Get a few of the groups to come to the front to read their sentences. The team that manages to write the most sentences will win. (10 – 15 minutes)

 Language Assessment: Photocopy the language assessment sheet on page 26 of the Assessment Pack. Give each student a copy to complete in order to check what they have learned over the course of the unit.

 Self Assessment: Photocopy the self assessment sheet on page 4 of the Assessment Pack. Give a copy to each student for them to complete on their own. Offer help where necessary.

Global Assessment: Complete the global assessment on page 5 of the Assessment Pack. Check whether the objectives set out at the start of the unit were achieved by your students. Keep a record to refer back to in coming units.

Interactive presentation. Use the Teacher's Multi-ROM to work with the Student's Book or with the Big Book Builder.

 **Bounce around: Art**

1 Make a finger puppet.

You will need:

card, glue stick,

tape, colored pencils

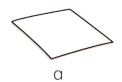

a

b

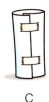

c

d

e

a.   Cut a strip of card for the body.

b/c.   Roll it up over your finger and tape it together.

d.   Draw eyes, a nose and a mouth on your puppet's face.

e.   Color your puppet. Paste or draw shapes to make clothes.

Write the name of your puppet.

2 Talk about your finger puppet.

What's he doing?

He's laughing.

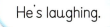

Talk about

unit 4 LESSON 1

 1 Listen and point. Say the words.
Track 15

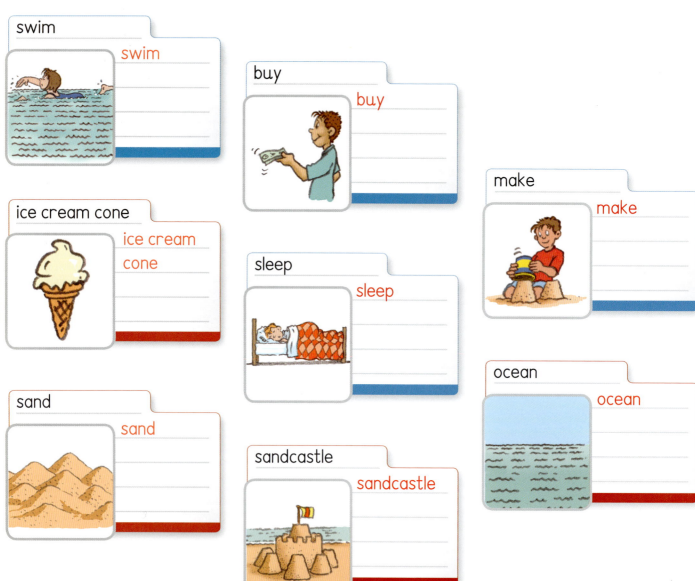

swim

swim

buy

buy

make

make

ice cream cone

ice cream
cone

sleep

sleep

ocean

ocean

sand

sand

sandcastle

sandcastle

2 Write the words in exercise 1.

unit 4

Lesson 1

Vocabulary presentation

Materials: track 15, sheet of paper, photo or picture of a beach scene, Activity Resource Book page 11, scissors, glue, colored pencils

Lesson objectives: Learn vocabulary about the beach

New vocabulary: *swim, buy, make, sleep, ice cream cone, ocean, sand, sandcastle*

Global assessment indicators

a Student works well in teams

b Student presents work with care

c Student respects classroom rules

d Student is interested in learning

Global Assessment ✓

1 Bounce into action!

- Stick the photo or picture of a beach scene on the board. Elicit from students any words they know connected to beaches and vacations.
- Discuss their ideas and write the words they already know on the board.

2 Exercise 1

 track 15

Listen and point. Say the words.

- Point to each picture in the book and say *Listen and point.* Play track 15 and encourage students to point to the pictures as they hear them.
- Say *Say the words.* Play the track again and press the pause button after each word so students can repeat them together.

3 Exercise 2

Write the words in exercise 1.

- Ask students to write down the words in their books.
- Go around the room helping and encouraging the students to say the words they are writing.

4 Word window (optional activity)

- Ask students to open their Activity Resource Book to page 11. Ask them to draw a beach scene in the box. They must include all the new words.
- Ask them to color in the sea and cut out the box along the dotted line.
- Encourage them to decorate the border of their drawing.
- Divide the class into pairs. Each student should show their picture to his/her partner and point and say the objects and actions using the new vocabulary.

5 Bounce on!

1 Write the verbs on the board. Give students enough time to memorize them and ask them to close their eyes. Erase one of the words. Ask them to open their eyes and say the missing word. Continue in this way until they have identified all the missing words. (5 – 10 minutes)

2 Divide the board in two sections: *ocean* and *sand.* Get one of the students to come to the front and say *Swim.* The student must go to the correct side of the board and perform the correct action. (5 – 10 minutes)

Multi-ROM task   Student's Multi-ROM

Ask students to complete the Unit 4 Lesson 1 activity on the Student's Multi-ROM to review the vocabulary they have learned.

Interactive presentation. Use the Teacher's Multi-ROM to work with the Student's Book or with the Big Book Builder.

T28

unit 4

Materials: track 16, colored pencils, blank sheets of paper for each student, Big Book Builder 2 pages 10 and 11

Lesson objectives:	Learn to talk about actions in the plural
Vocabulary review:	Beach vocabulary
New grammar:	*They're making sandcastles.*

1 Bounce into action!

- Divide the board into two with a wavy line. On one side write *Ocean* and on the other *Sand*.
- Say the vocabulary words. Students are to come to the front and write the word on the correct side of the board and do the action.

2 Exercise 1

Listen and number.

- Point to the picture of the beach and say *Listen and point*.
- Play track 16 and encourage students to point to the people.
- Play the track again and press the pause button after each sentence and ask students to repeat them.
- Ask them to number each picture.

3 Exercise 2

Match the sentences to the people in exercise 1.

- Ask students to identify the sentences with the people in the picture and match the number to the picture.
- Write *Today's grammar* on the board and ask students to copy it down.

> **Today's grammar**
>
> | They're | making sandcastles. |
> | | buying ice cream cones. |

4 Exercise 3

Write more sentences about the people in exercise 1.

- Ask students to point to other people in the picture and say sentences about them.
- Tell them to write the sentences down.

5 Exercise 4

Talk time. Draw two more people at the beach. Ask your friends what they are doing.

- Ask students to draw two people doing some sort of activity on the beach. Divide the class into pairs and ask them to take turns asking and answering questions about the people.

> **Optional Activity:**
>
> **Big Book Builder 2** pages 10 and 11, *On Vacation*. Do the activities suggested on pages xi to xix of this book.

6 Bounce on!

1. Write on the board *the in sand. playing They're (They're playing in the sand)*. Divide the class into groups and encourage them to work in teams to place the sentence in the correct order. (5 – 10 minutes)

2. Hand out the blank sheets of paper. Get them to draw a sandcastle and under the picture write *My sandcastle* and their name. Then ask them to come to the front and describe their sandcastle using the adjectives they have learned during the year. (10 – 15 minutes)

Home Study page 86

Write the following task instruction on the board and ask students to copy it in the space provided:

"Join the numbers to see the picture. Complete the sentences."

Interactive presentation. Use the Teacher's Multi-ROM to work with the Student's Book or with the Big Book Builder.

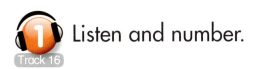 Listen and number.

Today's grammar
They're making sandcastles.

2 Match the sentences to the people in exercise 1.

1 Look at the children. They're buying ice cream cones.	1
2 Look at the girls. They're laughing.	6
3 Look at the boys. They're playing in the sand.	4
4 Look at Mom and Jane. They're sleeping.	5
5 Look at the children. They're making sandcastles.	3
6 Look at the boys. They're swimming in the ocean.	2

3 Write more sentences about the people in exercise 1.

1 Look at Dad. _(students' own answers)_ .

2 _(students' own answers)_ .

4 Draw two more people at the beach.
Ask your friends what they are doing.

Talk time
What are they doing?
They're swimming.

1 Join the dots. Complete the questions and answers.

Today's grammar

What are they doing?
They're buying ice cream cones.

unit 4 LESSON 3

1 What are they doing?

They're __buying ice cream cones_____.

2 What are __they doing_____?

They're __building sandcastles_____.

3 __What are they doing_____?

__They're swimming_____.

Bounce back

to Unit 3 Unscramble the sentences.

1 he What's doing

__What's he doing_____?

2 isn't drinking He

__He isn't drinking_____.

3 eating a yogurt He's

__He's eating a yogurt_____.

30

Lesson 3
Grammar presentation

Materials: colored pencils, pictures of the beach words, non-transparent bag

Lesson objectives:	Learn to ask and answer questions about actions in the plural
Vocabulary review:	Beach vocabulary
Grammar review:	*What are they doing? They're sleeping.*

❶ Bounce into action!

- Check that students have completed and understood the task in the Home Study section on page 86. (Answers: p.167)
- Divide the class into two groups. Point to the first group and say *Swim*. The students are to pretend to be swimming. The other group is to say *They're swimming*.
- Point to the second group and say *Make sandcastles*. Encourage them to do the correct action to allow the other group to say *They're making sandcastles*.
- Continue in this way until you have practiced all the words; make sure you alternate the groups.

❷ Exercise 1

Join the dots. Complete the questions and answers.

- Get two students to come to the front and whisper to them that they should pretend to be sleeping. Point to them and ask the class *What are they doing?* Encourage them to answer together *They're sleeping*. Model the new structure again and get students to repeat the sentences, first together and then individually.
- Write *Today's grammar* on the board and ask students to copy it down.

> **Today's grammar**
> **What are they doing?**
>
> **They're** | sleeping.
> | making sandcastles.

- Ask students to join the dots and write the questions and answers in their books.
- Go around the room helping and encouraging them.

❸ Bounce back. Unscramble the sentences.
(Review activity)

- Read the sentences with the students. Ask them to put the sentences in the correct order.
- Go around correcting the students' work.
- Get several students to come to the front to read the sentences aloud.

❹ Bounce on!

1 Divide the class into two teams. Place the pictures of the beach words in a non-transparent bag. Get a student from the first team to come to the front of the class, take a picture out of the bag and say the word. Then ask him/her to make a sentence using the word. If the student says a correct sentence, he/she will win a point for the team. (10 – 15 minutes)

2 Divide the class into pairs. Ask the students to show their pictures to their partners and take turns asking and answering *What are they doing? They're buying ice cream cones*. Go around helping the pairs with their pronunciation. (5 minutes)

Interactive presentation. Use the Teacher's Multi-ROM to work with the Student's Book or with the Big Book Builder.

T30

unit 4

Lesson 4

Write about . . . a vacation at the beach.

Materials: a sheet of paper for each student, colored pencils, pictures showing the beach, clothing and footwear words

Lesson objectives:	Read and write a postcard
Vocabulary review:	Beach, clothing and footwear vocabulary
Grammar review:	*I'm wearing . . . / It's . . . / They're . . .*

1 Bounce into action!

- Ask one of the students to leave the room. Tell the rest of the class *Swim in the ocean* and encourage them to do the action when the student comes back into the room.
- Get one of the students in the room to ask the student who has come back into the room to say *What are they doing?* The student who has come back is to answer *They're swimming in the ocean*.
- Ask another student to leave the room and repeat the same steps.

2 Exercise 1

Read the postcard from Mandy.

- Look at the picture with the students and say *Look! It's a postcard!* Point to the people and ask each time *What are they doing?* Encourage the students to answer.
- Read the postcard with students. Ask a few students to read the sentences for the whole class.
- Ask comprehension questions to check that they have understood, for example, *Is it cold? / What is Mandy wearing? / What are Andy and Mary Jo doing?* etc.

3 Exercise 2

Write a postcard with the words from the box.

- Explain to students that they are going to write a postcard. Ask them to read the words in the box.
- Read the greeting and model the steps to follow. Read the options in the box aloud until they find the correct word. Ask students to read the full sentence *Today is Friday*. Write it on the board.
- Repeat the same steps with the second sentence and then ask students to finish writing the sentences on their own.
- Go around helping them.

4 Bounce on!

1 Place the pictures of the beach, clothing and footwear words around the room. Write the following words on the board: *beach, clothes, shoes*. Ask one of the students to come to the front to find the picture of the word you are saying and place it under the correct word. Continue in this way until you have used all the words. After this you can ask them to choose a word from each column and write a sentence. (15 minutes)

2 Hand a sheet of paper to each student and ask them to draw a picture on the front of the postcard they have just written. (10 minutes)

Home Study page 87

Write the following task instructions on the board and ask students to copy them in the space provided:

"Design a postcard about Sunny Beach. Then write three sentences using the words in the box."

Interactive presentation. Use the Teacher's Multi-ROM to work with the Student's Book or with the Big Book Builder.

a vacation at the beach.

1 Read the postcard from Mandy.

Dear Grandma and Grandpa,
Today is Tuesday. It's hot and
sunny. I'm wearing green shorts
and a yellow T-shirt. I'm wearing
my brown sandals. Andy and Mary
Jo are swimming in the ocean.
Lucy and Neil are making sandcastles.
Mom and Dad are sleeping on the
sand. I love vacations!
See you soon,
Mandy

2 Write a postcard with the words from the box.

> are buying ice cream cones   Friday   blue shorts   Dear
>
> hot and sunny   are drinking sodas   vacations   a red T-shirt
>
> black sandals   Love   are laughing

_Dear_____ Grandma and Grandpa,

Today is _Friday_____. It's

_hot and sunny_____.

I'm wearing _blue shorts____ and _a red T-shirt_____.

I'm wearing _black sandals_____. Andy and Mary Jo

_are drinking sodas_____. Lucy and Neil

_are laughing_____. Mom and Dad _are buying_____

_ice cream cones_____. I love _vacations_____!

_Love_____, _____.

1 Listen and point. Say the words.

Track 17

hold

dance

kiss

feed

trumpet

trainer

seal

rope

2 Complete the words and draw pictures.

1

1 The monkeys are h old i n g bananas.

2

2 The dogs are playing the t ru m p e t.

3

3 The s e a l s are swimming.

4

4 The trainers are k i ss i n g the seals.

Lesson 5

Vocabulary presentation

Materials: tracks 04 and 17, Big Book Builder 2 pages 10 and 11

Lesson objectives:	Learn vocabulary about entertainment/shows
New vocabulary:	*hold, dance, kiss, feed, trumpet, trainer, seal, rope*

1 Bounce into action!

- Check that students have completed and understood the task in the Home Study section on page 87. (Answers: p.167)
- Sing the song *Months are fun to say!* from unit 1 Lesson 4. Divide the class into six groups. Play track 04. Ask each group to sing two lines.
- Point to the groups one by one and sing the song in the correct order.
- Point to the groups randomly and sing the song in any order.

2 Exercise 1

Listen and point. Say the words.

- Point to the pictures of the new words in the book and say *Listen and point.*
- Play track 17. Ask students to point to the pictures as they hear them on the track.
- Say *Say the words.* Play the track again and press the pause button after each word so students can repeat the words together.
- When students can say the words confidently, encourage them to say the words individually.

3 Exercise 2

Complete the words and draw pictures.

- Explain to students that they must read the sentences and complete the missing letters.
- Read the first sentence with the students and encourage them to say the word.
- Get one of the students to come to the front and write the word on the board and then ask the students to complete the exercise on their own.
- Ask them to draw the corresponding pictures.
- Go around the room helping and correcting their work.

> **Optional Activity:**
> **Big Book Builder 2** pages 10 and 11, *On Vacation.* Do the activities suggested on pages xi to xix of this book.

4 Bounce on!

1 Play *Hangman!* Divide the class into two teams. The students in one team are to think of a word. Ask one student from that team to come to the front and draw a dash for each of the letters in the word. The other team is to try to guess the word by saying letters of the alphabet. If the letter is in the word, the student at the front must write the letter in the word; if the letter is not in the word, he/she must draw part of the person being hanged (i.e. head, body and limbs). When the team guesses the word or the other team has finished drawing the hangman, the teams are to change roles. (5 – 10 minutes)

2 Divide the class into two teams. Write one of the new words on the board, for example, *seal.* Have a student come to the front and get him/her to write a word on the board. They can write, *The seals are dancing. / The seals are eating. / The seals are swimming.* Any student writing a correct sentence will win a point for their team. (10 minutes)

> **Multi-ROM task** Student's Multi-ROM
>
> Ask students to complete the Unit 4 Lesson 5 activity on the Student's Multi-ROM to review the vocabulary they have learned.

> **Interactive presentation.** Use the Teacher's Multi-ROM to work with the Student's Book or with the Big Book Builder.

Grammar and song presentation

Materials: track 18, Activity Resource Book page 25, Big Book Builder 2 pages 10 and 11

Lesson objectives:	Learn to say what people are not doing in the third person Learn the song *Join the fun!*
New grammar:	*They aren't . . .*

1 Bounce into action!

- Get several students to come to the front and whisper to them *Hold a rope*. Ask them to mime the corresponding action. The other students must guess the action and say *They are holding a rope*.
- Continue practicing the structure and vocabulary with various students.

2 Exercise 1

Look at the pictures. Correct the sentences.

- Draw a picture on the board of two children dancing. Say *They are sleeping*. Get students to correct the statement by saying *They aren't sleeping. They're dancing*.
- Look at the photos and read the sentences with the students. Encourage them to correct the sentences orally and ask them to write them in their books.
- Write *Today's grammar* on the board and ask students to copy it down.

Today's grammar	
They aren't	eating fish. dancing.

3 Exercise 2

 ### Sing the song: *Join the fun!*

track 18

- Play track 18 and encourage students to mime the actions.
- Model each line in the song and get students to repeat the lines together.
- Play the track again and sing the song together.
- Ask students to open their Activity Resource Book to page 25 and do the activities.

Optional Activity:

Big Book Builder 2 pages 10 and 11, *On Vacation*. Do the activities suggested on pages xi to xix of this book.

4 Bounce on!

1 Look at the pictures with the students. Explain to them that you are going to say sentences. If the sentence is correct, they must stand up. If the sentence is incorrect, they must place their hands on their head and correct it. Point to the first picture and say *The dolphins are sleeping*. They must raise their hands to their head and say *The dolphins aren't sleeping*. Repeat the steps with other sentences. (5 – 10 minutes)

2 Write the lines of the song in any order on the board. Divide the class into groups and ask them to put the song in the correct order. The first team completing the task correctly will win. Encourage the whole class to sing the song with the track. (10 minutes)

 Home Study page 88

Write the following task instructions on the board and ask students to copy them in the space provided:

"Look at the pictures. Complete the sentences with *are* or *aren't*. Circle *T* if the sentence is true or *F* if the sentence is false."

Multi-ROM task Student's Multi-ROM

Ask the students to listen to the song *Join the fun!*, track 18, at home until they have memorized it.

 **Interactive presentation.** Use the Teacher's Multi-ROM to work with the Student's Book or with the Big Book Builder.

Look at the pictures.
Correct the sentences.

 **Today's grammar**

They aren't eating fish.

1 The dolphins are feeding the trainers.

They aren't <u>feeding the trainers</u>.

The trainers are feeding the dolphins.

2 The trainers are dancing.

<u>They aren't dancing</u>.

<u>The dolphins are dancing</u>.

3 The trainers are holding trumpets.

<u>They aren't holding trumpets</u>.

<u>The seals are holding trumpets</u>.

Track 18

Sing the song: Join the fun!

The children are playing,
The trainers are swimming,
The dolphins are singing a song.
Come to the show,
Join the fun!
Let's sing the dolphin song!

The children are playing,
The trainers are swimming,
The seals are playing a tune.
Come to the show,
Join in the fun!
Let's sing the seal tune!

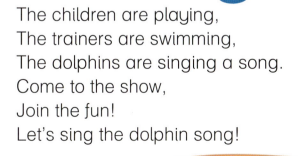
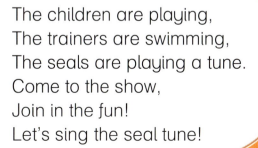

Listen and read. **The lucky dolphins.**

Track 19

1

John and Jamie are at the dolphin show with Mom and Dad. They're having fun. It's lunchtime and they're eating fish sandwiches.

2

"Look at the dolphins, Jamie. They're playing basketball. And look, they're dancing!" says John.

3

Where's Jamie? He isn't sitting with Mom and Dad and he isn't playing with John.
What's he doing?

4

"There's Jamie!" says John. "Look, he's feeding the dolphins. They're eating fish sandwiches! Take a picture, Dad!"

2 Answer the question. What's Dad doing?

He's taking a picture _____.

34

unit 4

Lesson 7

Read a story

Materials: track 19, cardboard, Big Book Builder 2 pages 10 and 11

Lesson objectives:	Consolidate the unit's vocabulary through a story
Vocabulary review:	Shows
Grammar review:	*They're . . .*

1 Bounce into action!

- Check that students have completed and understood the task in the Home Study section on page 88. (Answers: p. 167)
- Explain to the students that they are going to listen to a story.
- Look at the pictures. Point to the people and animals and ask *What are they doing?* Encourage them to answer.
- Ask students what they think the story will be about and write some of their sentences on the board.

2 Exercise 1

Listen and read. *The lucky dolphins.*

- Say *Listen* and play track 19. Encourage the students to point to the pictures as they hear them during the story.
- Play the track again. Encourage them to read the text as they are hearing it.
- Ask them to say what they think the story is about. Point to their suggestions on the board and talk about the similarities to the story they have just heard.
- Talk about the actions of the dolphins and Jamie.
- Read the story with the students. Ask a few students to read the sentences for the whole class.

3 Exercise 2

Answer the question. What's Dad doing?

- Ask *What's Dad doing?* Encourage them to answer *He's taking a picture.*
- Ask students to write the sentence in their books.

> **Optional Activity:**
>
> **Big Book Builder 2** pages 10 and 11, *On Vacation*. Do the activities suggested on pages xi to xix of this book.

4 Bounce on!

1 Divide the class into pairs. Encourage them to take turns asking and answering questions about the actions of Jamie, his family and the dolphins. (5 – 10 minutes)

2 Write sentences from the story on cardboard. Cut the story into strips and put them on the board in any order. Divide the class into teams and ask them to put the story in the correct order. (10 minutes)

Multi-ROM task   Student's Multi-ROM

Ask the students to listen to the story *The lucky dolphins*, track 19, at home until they can perform a role-play during the next class.

Interactive presentation. Use the Teacher's Multi-ROM to work with the Student's Book or with the Big Book Builder.

T34

Lesson 8

Bounce around: Social Studies

Materials: pictures of water, houses, countryside, factories, an animal, a plant and a person, cardboard, colored pencils, two different magnets, track 19, Assessment Pack pages 4, 5 and 27

Lesson objectives:	Learn through social studies
	Develop critical thinking and reasoning
	Review the vocabulary learned during the unit
	Vocabulary expansion
Vocabulary review:	Plants, animals
New vocabulary:	*water, humans, home, countryside, factories*

1 Bounce into action!

- Ask students to come to the front and role-play the story *The lucky dolphins*, track 19, in groups of four.

2 Exercise 1

 Read and match the photographs to their correct places.

- Place the pictures of water on the board and ask the students what they see. Place the pictures of the person, plants and animals on the board and ask them why water is important for human beings.
- Then get them to read and do the activity.

3 Exercise 2

Write three things you need water for.

- Place the picture of the house and ask students why people use water at home. Write their suggestions on the board. Do the same thing with the pictures of the countryside and the factory.
- Then ask students to choose from the board three reasons why they need water and copy them down in their books.

4 Exercise 3

Talk about water.

- Ask students to talk about the importance of water and its uses, and ask them about how they can save water at home.
- Then, divide the class into pairs and ask them to talk about how they could save water at school.

5 Bounce on!

1 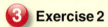 Divide the class into groups of four students. Hand out the cards and ask them to draw pictures about actions that can help to save water at home and at school. Ask some of the students to come to the front to present their work. Then display the cards throughout the school to increase the students' awareness about using and preserving water. (15 – 20 minutes)

2 Ask students to form teams and write four questions and answers about the use and preservation of water. Collect the questions and play a mini-marathon with the students. Divide the class into two teams. Draw ten squares on the board plus start and finish lines. The magnets will show the progress of the two teams. Ask a question to the first team; if they answer correctly advance their magnet one square. Continue asking questions until the first team reaches the finish line. (15 – 20 minutes)

Language Assessment: Photocopy the language assessment sheet on page 27 of the Assessment Pack. Give each student a copy to complete in order to check what they have learned over the course of the unit.

 Self Assessment: Photocopy the self assessment sheet on page 4 of the Assessment Pack. Give a copy to each student for them to complete on their own. Offer help where necessary.

Global Assessment: Complete the global assessment on page 5 of the Assessment Pack. Check whether the objectives set out at the start of the unit were achieved by your students. Keep a record to refer back to in coming units.

 **around:** Social Studies

1 Read and match the photographs to their correct places.

Water is vital for humans, plants and animals. It is used in the home, in the countryside and in factories.

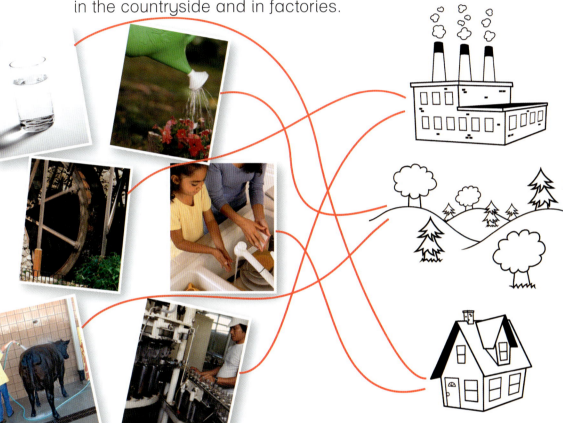

2 Write three things you need water for.

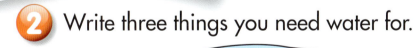

(students' own answers)
_____
_____

3 Talk about water.

I need water to drink.

Talk about

 1 Listen and point. Say the words.

Track 20

do homework

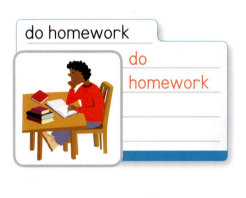

do homework

watch television

watch television

clean your room

clean your room

call a friend

call a friend

listen to music

listen to music

water a plant

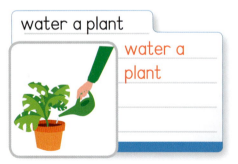

water a plant

make a snack

make a snack

ride a bicycle

ride a bicycle

2 Write the words in exercise 1.

36

unit 5

Lesson 1

Vocabulary presentation

Materials: tracks 18 and 20, Activity Resource Book page 13, colored pencils, scissors

Lesson objectives:	Learn expressions relating to free time
New vocabulary:	*do homework, watch television, listen to music, clean your room, call a friend, ride a bicycle, water a plant, make a snack*

Global assessment indicators

a Student works well in teams
b Student presents work with care
c Student respects classroom rules
d Student is interested in learning

Global Assessment ✓

① Bounce into action!

- Divide the class into two groups. Play track 18. Sing *Join the fun!* from unit 4 Lesson 6. Get each group to sing one verse; then get them to sing together. Play the track if students need help remembering the song.

② Exercise 1

track 20

Listen and point. Say the words.

- Point to each picture in the book, say the words and do the corresponding action.
- Point to the pictures one by one and get students to do the action.
- Say *Listen and point*. Play track 20 and encourage students to point to the corresponding pictures.
- Say *Say the words*. Play the track again and press the pause button after each phrase so students can repeat the words all together.

③ Exercise 2

Write the words in exercise 1.

- Ask students to write down the phrases.
- Go around the room helping and encouraging the students to say the phrases while they are writing them.

④ Word window (optional activity)

- Ask students to open their Activity Resource Book to page 13. Ask them to write the verbs on one half of the cards (*do, watch,* etc.) and then draw and write words on the other half (*homework, television, music,* etc.). Tell them to color in and cut out the cards.
- Divide the class into pairs. Get students to place their cards facedown, then take turns turning over the cards to form pairs of verbs and drawings. The student with the most pairs wins the game.

⑤ Bounce on!

1 Ask one student to come to the front. Whisper to him/her *Call a friend*. The student should act out the phrase and the others must guess the action. The student guessing correctly comes to the front. Repeat the same steps with the other words. (5 – 10 minutes)

2 Play *Bounce Says* with the new phrases. If you say *Bounce says* students must do the action. If you do not say *Bounce says*, they must remain still. (5 – 10 minutes)

Multi-ROM task   Student's Multi-ROM

Ask students to complete the Unit 5 Lesson 1 activity on the Student's Multi-ROM to review the vocabulary they have learned.

Interactive presentation. Use the Teacher's Multi-ROM to work with the Student's Book or with the Big Book Builder.

T36

Lesson 2

Grammar presentation

Materials: track 21

Lesson objectives:	Use expressions about free time
Vocabulary review:	Free time expressions
New grammar:	*I'm calling my friends.*

① Bounce into action!

- Instruct and encourage students to do the action. Say *Girls, listen to the music.* The girls are to pretend to be listening to music. Say *Boys, water a plant.* The boys are to pretend to be watering a plant. Every now and then say *Children, ride a bike* and get the whole class to do the corresponding action.
- Continue in this way and practice all the phrases.

② Exercise 1

Complete the sentences.

- Encourage students to complete the sentences.
- Go around the room helping them.
- Write *Today's grammar* on the board and ask students to copy it down.

Today's grammar

I'm	calling my friends.
	watching television.

Audioscript:
Boy: I'm listening to music. Girl: I'm cleaning my room.
Boy: I'm calling my friend. Girl: I'm watering the plants.
Boy: I'm riding a bicycle. Girl: I'm watching television.
Girl: I'm doing my homework. Boy: I'm making a snack.

③ Exercise 2

Listen and check.

- Say *Listen and check* and play track 21. Get students to listen carefully and correct their sentences.
- Play the track again and check the work with students.

④ Exercise 3

Talk time. Mime an action. Tell your friends.

- Say *It's talk time!* Divide the class into pairs. Tell them to take turns miming the actions and saying the sentences.
- Check that students are working properly and help them with their pronunciation.

⑤ Bounce on!

1 Ask students to draw themselves doing their favorite activity. Have some of the students come to the front to show their pictures and describe them. Ask them to write a sentence under their picture. Display the pictures around the room. (10 minutes)

2 Divide the class into four or five groups; get them to stand in a line. The first student from each group must show their picture and say a sentence. The first student must then point to the next student, and continue in this way following the same steps. Continue in this way until all students have had their turn. Decorate the walls of the room with the pictures. (5 – 10 minutes)

Home Study
page 89

Write the following task instruction on the board and ask students to copy it in the space provided:

"Read and follow the instructions. Complete the sentence."

Interactive presentation. Use the Teacher's Multi-ROM to work with the Student's Book or with the Big Book Builder.

1 Complete the sentences.

Today's grammar

I'm calling my friends.

1 I'm <u>listening to</u>
<u>music</u>.

4 I'm <u>watering</u>
<u>the plants</u>.

2 I'm <u>cleaning</u>
<u>my room</u>.

5 I'm <u>riding</u>
<u>a bicycle</u>.

7 I'm <u>doing my</u>
<u>homework</u>.

3 I'm <u>calling</u>
<u>a friend</u>.

6 I'm <u>watching</u>
<u>television</u>.

8 I'm <u>making</u>
<u>a snack</u>.

2 Listen and check.

Track 21

3 Mime an action. Tell your friends.

Talk time

I'm making a snack.

 1 Listen to the conversation. Number the sentences in the correct order.

Track 22

Today's grammar

What are you doing?
I'm making a snack.

Kelly:	A snack?	5
Simon:	I'm making a snack.	4
Kelly:	Apple cookies! Wow! Wait for me!	7
Simon:	Hi, Kelly. What are you doing?	2
Kelly:	Hello?	1
Simon:	Yes, I'm making apple cookies.	6
Kelly:	Hi, Simon. I'm listening to music. What are you doing?	3

 2 Act out the conversation with a friend.

Track 23

Sing the song: Free time

Free time, free time,
What shall I do?
I love my free time,
How about you?

I'm listening to music,
Hey, you can, too!
I'm watching basketball,
How about you?

I'm watering plants,
Hey, you can, too!
I'm riding my bicycle,
How about you?

Lesson 3

Grammar and song presentation

Materials: tracks 22 and 23, Activity Resource Book page 26

Lesson objectives:	Learn to ask and answer questions about free time activities
	Learn the song *Free time*
New grammar:	*What are you doing? I'm feeding the dogs.*

1 Bounce into action!

- Check that students have completed and understood the task in the Home Study section on page 89. (Answers: p.167)
- Divide the class into groups. Assign a color to each group. Say *Blue team, make a snack.* Students on the blue team should mime the action.
- Continue in this way with all the expressions and all the groups.

2 Exercise 1

track 22

Listen to the conversation. Number the sentences in the correct order.

- Ask one student to do an action and say *What are they doing?* Encourage them to answer. Have the whole class repeat the sentences. Continue in this way.
- Write *Today's grammar* on the board and ask students to copy it down.

Today's grammar
What are you doing?   I'm . . .

- Explain to them that they are going to listen to a phone conversation. Say *Listen* and play track 22.
- Play the track again and ask them to number the sentences.
- Play it again and check their work.

3 Exercise 2

Act out the conversation with a friend.

- Divide the class into pairs and ask them to act out the dialogue.
- Go around helping the pairs with their pronunciation.

4 Exercise 3

track 23

Sing the song: *Free time*

- Explain to students they are going to listen to a song. Say *Listen* and play track 23.
- Play the track again and encourage students to mime the actions.
- Model each line of the song and get students to repeat the lines together.
- Play the track again and sing the song together.
- Ask students to open their Activity Resource Book to page 26 and do the activities.

5 Bounce on!

1 Divide the class into groups of four. Ask them to think of other verses for different actions and then write them down. Ask the students to read their verses aloud. Sing the song with the new verses. (5 – 10 minutes)

2 Divide the class into pairs and ask them to practice the dialogue. Get some of the pairs to come to the front and act out the dialogue. (10 minutes)

Multi-ROM task   Student's Multi-ROM

Ask the students to listen to the song *Free time*, track 23, at home until they have memorized it.

Interactive presentation. Use the Teacher's Multi-ROM to work with the Student's Book or with the Big Book Builder.

Lesson 4

Grammar presentation

Materials: track 23, Big Book Builder 2 pages 12 and 13

Lesson objectives:	Learn to use free time expressions in the negative
Vocabulary review:	Free time expressions
New grammar:	*I'm not making a snack.*

① Bounce into action!

- Sing the song *Free time*, track 23. Encourage students to mime the actions.
- Add the verses written by students during the previous class.

② Exercise 1

Read. Answer the questions.

- Draw the picture of a television, a sandwich and a few musical notes on the board. Point to the television and say *I'm not watching television*, and cross it out at the same time. Point to the sandwich and say *I'm not making a snack*, crossing it out at the same time. Point to the musical notes, do the corresponding mime and say *I'm listening to music*.
- Repeat the sentences and get the students to say them together and then individually.
- Draw other pictures on the board and continue presenting the new structure in the same way.
- Write *Today's grammar* on the board and ask students to copy it down.

Today's grammar

I'm not	making a snack.
	watching television.

- Read the sentences with students. Do the first riddle together.
- Have one of the students come to the front and write the answer on the board, and then ask them to complete the exercise on their own.

③ Bounce back. Look at the pictures and write sentences. (Review activity)

- Look at the pictures with students and review the words *sleeping* and *dancing*.
- Write the first sentence together with the students and then ask them to complete the exercise on their own.

> **Optional Activity:**
> **Big Book Builder 2** pages 12 and 13, *Numbers*. Do the activities suggested on pages xi to xix of this book.

④ Bounce on!

1 Divide the class into pairs. Ask them to read the sentences again in their books and to write another riddle about one of the eight children in the pictures. Go around helping and encouraging the pairs. (10 minutes)

2 Form groups of two pairs. Ask them to take turns saying their riddle and get the other pair to point to the corresponding picture. Go around helping students with their pronunciation. (5 – 10 minutes)

Home Study page 90

Write the following task instructions on the board and ask students to copy them in the space provided:

"Read about what the children are saying. Write and draw a picture about something you are saying."

Interactive presentation. Use the Teacher's Multi-ROM to work with the Student's Book or with the Big Book Builder.

1 Read. Answer the questions.

 Sally  Eddie  Jennifer  Mark

1
I'm not watering the plants.
I'm not calling my friends.
I'm not making a snack.
Who am I?

Eddie_____.

2
I'm not making a snack.
I'm not watching television.
I'm not calling my friends.
Who am I?

Mark_____.

Dan  Dawn  Nicola  Rory

3
I'm not riding my bicycle.
I'm not watering the plants.
I'm not listening to music.
Who am I?

Nicola_____.

4
I'm not cleaning my room.
I'm not watering the plants.
I'm not riding my bicycle.
Who am I?

Dan_____.

Bounce back

to Unit 4 Look at the pictures and write sentences.

 ✗ **1** He _isn't sleeping_____.

 ✓ **2** He _'s listening to music_____.

1 Listen and point. Say the words.
Track 24

twenty
20

twenty-one
21

twenty-two
22

twenty-three
23

twenty-four
24

twenty-five
25

twenty-six
26

twenty-seven
27

twenty-eight
28

twenty-nine
29

thirty
30

forty
40

fifty
50

sixty
60

seventy
70

eighty
80

ninety
90

one hundred
100

 2 Listen and write.
Track 25

1 ___24 twenty-four___

2 ___29 twenty-nine___

3 ___30 thirty___

4 ___50 fifty___

5 ___100 one hundred___

6 ___21 twenty-one___

Vocabulary presentation

Materials: tracks 24 and 25, card, photocopy of a 10-by-10 grid for each student, Big Book Builder 2 pages 12 and 13

Lesson objectives:	Learn numbers from twenty to one hundred
New vocabulary:	*twenty, twenty-one, twenty-two, twenty-three, twenty-four, twenty-five, twenty-six, twenty-seven, twenty-eight, twenty-nine, thirty, forty, fifty, sixty, seventy, eighty, ninety, one hundred*

1 Bounce into action!

- Check that students have completed and understood the task in the Home Study section on page 90. (Answers: p.167)
- Clap rhythmically and count from 1 to 20. Encourage students to imitate you. Increase the speed at which you are saying the numbers.
- Clap and get students to say the numbers without your help.
- Get students to say the numbers in reverse order.

2 Exercise 1

track 24

Listen and point. Say the words.

- Point to the numbers in the book. Say *Listen and point* and play track 24.
- Get the students to point to the numbers as they hear them on the track.
- Say *Say the words*. Play the track again and press the pause button after each number so students can repeat them together and then individually.

3 Exercise 2

track 25

Listen and write.

- Explain to students that they are going to hear some numbers and must write them down. Say *Listen* and play track 25. Press the pause button after each number to allow students to write them down.

- Play the track again and encourage students to check their work.
- Invite some of the students to come to the front and write the numbers on the board. Ask the class to say each number together.

Audioscript:
24, 29, 22, 23, 27, 21, 30, 25, 20, 28

Optional Activity:
Big Book Builder 2 pages 12 and 13, *Numbers*. Do the activities suggested on pages xi to xix of this book.

4 Bounce on!

1 Hand one of the photocopies to each student and say *Let's count to a hundred!* Draw a model of the photocopy on the card. Show them how to write the number 1 to 10 along the first row, from 11 to 20 along the second row and so on until they reach 100. Encourage them to say the numbers as they are writing them. (10 minutes)

2 Ask students to point to the numbers on their grids and count from 1 to 100. Point to the column on the right, and count from 10 to 100. The grid will help students to visualize the numbers and therefore remember them more easily. (5 – 10 minutes)

Multi-ROM task   Student's Multi-ROM

Ask students to complete the Unit 5 Lesson 5 activity on the Student's Multi-ROM to review the vocabulary they have learned.

Interactive presentation. Use the Teacher's Multi-ROM to work with the Student's Book or with the Big Book Builder.

Lesson 6

Grammar presentation

Materials: the number grid (1 to 100) from the previous class, track 26, Big Book Builder 2 pages 12 and 13, a small bag

Lesson objectives:	Learn to ask about the quantity of objects
Vocabulary review:	Numbers 1 to 100
New grammar:	*How many crayons does he have?*

1 Bounce into action!

- Place the grid with numbers 1 to 100 on the board. Point to the numbers and count together from one to one hundred.
- Point to the numbers to count to one hundred by increments of five (five, ten, etc.)
- Point to the right-hand column and count to one hundred, ten by ten.

2 Exercise 1

Circle the correct number.

- Get one of the students to come to the front and give him/her three pencils. Ask the class *How many pencils does he have?* Count the pencils with the class and say *He has three.* Model the question again and get students to repeat it together several times.
- Write *Today's grammar* on the board and ask students to copy it down.

Today's grammar

How many	crayons	does he have?
	books	

- Explain that Ricky has many things.
- Write the first problem on the board and show students how to solve it. Say *Thirty times two equals …* and encourage them to reply. Then say *Sixty minus five equals …* and wait for students to solve the problem.
- Ask students to solve the problems and provide the correct answers.

3 Exercise 2

Listen and check.

- Say *Listen and check your answers.* Play track 26 and get students to correct their answers.
- Play the track again and correct the problems with students.

Audioscript:

Ricky Rich: I love my free time! I have lots of things. I have 55 crayons. I have 43 balls. I have 50 books. I have 34 videos. I have 52 CDs.

4 Exercise 3

Write another math problem about Ricky's pens.

- Ask students to write and solve another problem.

Optional Activity:

Big Book Builder 2 pages 12 and 13, *Numbers*. Do the activities suggested on pages xi to xix of this book.

5 Bounce on!

1 Ask students to think about a mathematical problem and to write it down on a piece of paper. Collect the pieces of paper and put them in a bag. Get one of the students to come to the front and take one of the problems out of the bag. Ask him/her to read the problem aloud and then solve it. Repeat the same steps and ask several other students to come to the front. (10 – 15 minutes)

2 Divide the class into teams. Ask a member from each team to come to the front. Say a number from 1 to 100 and ask the children to write it on the board. The first child to do it correctly will win a point for his/her team. (5 – 10 minutes)

Home Study page 91

Write the following task instructions on the board and ask students to copy them in the space provided:

"Match the words to the corresponding numbers. Write the numbers in the correct order. Write the next number."

Interactive presentation. Use the Teacher's Multi-ROM to work with the Student's Book or with the Big Book Builder.

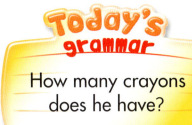

1 Circle the correct number.

Ricky Rich loves free time activities. He has lots of things.

1 How many crayons does he have?

He has 30 x 2 – 5.   25   65   (55)

2 How many balls does he have?

He has 20 x 4 – 40 + 3.   (43)   34   83

3 How many books does he have?

He has 100 – 90 x 5.   60   70   (50)

4 How many videos does he have?

He has 80 – 50 + 5 – 1.   43   (34)   46

5 How many CDs does he have?

He has 95 – 70 x 2 + 2.   (52)   62   72

 2 Listen and check.

Track 26

3 Write another math problem about Ricky's pens.

He has __(students' own answers)__.

Write about what you are doing.

1 Read the e-mail to Becky Bounce.

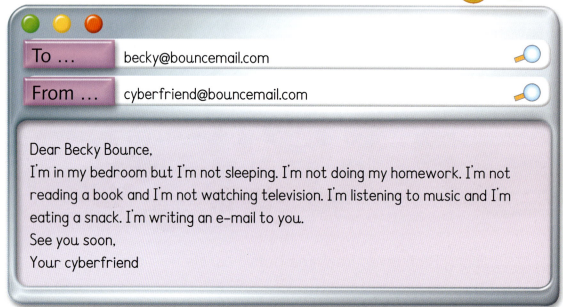

To … becky@bouncemail.com

From … cyberfriend@bouncemail.com

Dear Becky Bounce,
I'm in my bedroom but I'm not sleeping. I'm not doing my homework. I'm not reading a book and I'm not watching television. I'm listening to music and I'm eating a snack. I'm writing an e-mail to you.
See you soon,
Your cyberfriend

2 Write an e-mail to a friend.

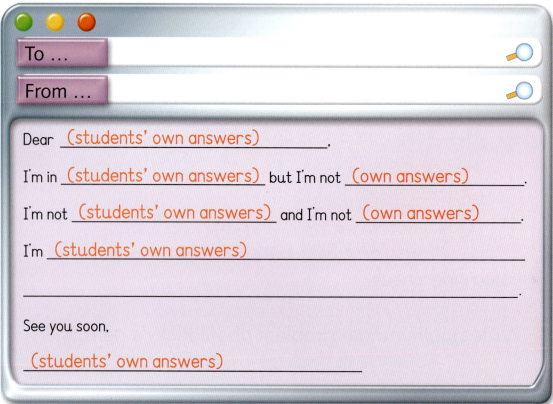

To …

From …

Dear (students' own answers) ,

I'm in (students' own answers) but I'm not (own answers) .

I'm not (students' own answers) and I'm not (own answers) .

I'm (students' own answers)

.

See you soon,

(students' own answers)

Lesson 7

Write about . . . what you are doing.

Materials: one sheet of paper for each student, colored pencils, Big Book Builder 2 pages 12 and 13, a ball

Lesson objectives:	Write an e-mail about what you are doing
Vocabulary review:	Free time expressions
Grammar review:	*I'm not . . . / I'm . . .*

1 Bounce into action!

- Check that students have completed and understood the task in the Home Study section on page 91. (Answers: p.167)
- Tell students that you are going to say sentences. Tell them to do the mime if you say you are doing something and not to move if you say you are not doing something. Say *I'm doing my homework*. They must pretend to be doing the task. Say *I'm not watching television*. They must remain still.

2 Exercise 1

Read the e-mail to Becky Bounce.

- Read the text with the students several times. Ask a few students to read the sentences for the whole class.
- Ask them what the cyberfriend of Becky is and is not doing.

> **Optional Activity:**
>
> **Big Book Builder 2** pages 12 and 13, *Numbers*. Do the activities suggested on pages xi to xix of this book.

3 Exercise 2

Write an e-mail to a friend.

- Explain to the students that they are going to write an electronic message.
- Draw a picture of the e-mail frame on the board. Ask students about the person they are going to write the e-mail to and get one of the students to come to the front to start the e-mail.
- Encourage them to say where they are and what they are and aren't doing. Write the sentences on the board.
- Ask them to choose a friend to write to and write the e-mail in their books.
- Go around the room helping and encouraging them.

4 Bounce on!

1 Hand a sheet of paper to each student and get them to draw themselves doing the activities they have just described. Divide the class into pairs. Students are to show their pictures to their partners and read their e-mail. (10 minutes)

2 Throw the ball to one of the students and say a sentence in the affirmative using the structure: *I'm.* The child receiving the ball must change the sentence to the negative. Continue in this way practicing the verbs and vocabulary seen up to now. (10 minutes)

> **Interactive presentation.** Use the Teacher's Multi-ROM to work with the Student's Book or with the Big Book Builder.

Lesson 8

Bounce around: Math

Materials: Assessment Pack pages 4, 5 and 28

Lesson objectives: Learn through mathematics
Develop logical/mathematical reasoning
Review the vocabulary learned during the unit

Vocabulary review: Numbers

① Bounce into action!

- Ask students to pay attention. Get them to do a series of mental calculations. Say *Twenty-five times three minus four plus seven equals seventy-eight.* Continue reviewing the numbers in the same way.
- Have the students think and say similar calculations.

② Exercise 1

Look at the jump results. Complete the totals for each person.

- Look at the pictures and encourage the children to say the number of points for each person.
- Ask them to write the total number of points.
- Go around the room checking that the students are doing the activity correctly.

③ Exercise 2

Record the results in a graph.

- Ask the students to record the results in a graph. Explain to them how they should complete it correctly.

- Go around the room checking that the students are working correctly.

④ Exercise 3

Talk about the results.

- Ask the students to form pairs to talk about their results. Encourage them to ask and answer questions and start a dialogue.

⑤ Bounce on!

1 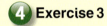 Play *Hangman* with the words for the numbers from 1 to 100. Divide the class into two teams. Get one member from each team to come to the front. One must draw as many dashes as there are letters in the word they are trying to get the other group to guess. If the other team says a letter that is in the word, he/she must write it in the correct position. If the letter is not in the word, they are to draw part of the hangman. The team guessing the most words wins. (5 – 10 minutes)

2 Tell the students that you are going to count all together. Each student must say a number. When someone says a multiple of ten, everyone must stand up; turn around, say the number, then sit down. Continue in this way until you reach one hundred. (10 minutes)

Language Assessment: Photocopy the language assessment sheet on page 28 of the Assessment Pack. Give each student a copy to complete in order to check what they have learned over the course of the unit.

 Self Assessment: Photocopy the self assessment sheet on page 4 of the Assessment Pack. Give a copy to each student for them to complete on their own. Offer help where necessary.

Global Assessment: Complete the global assessment on page 5 of the Assessment Pack. Check whether the objectives set out at the start of the unit were achieved by your students. Keep a record to refer back to in coming units.

Interactive presentation. Use the Teacher's Multi-ROM to work with the Student's Book or with the Big Book Builder.

Bounce around: Math

1 Look at the jump results. Complete the totals for each person.

NAME	First Round	Second Round	Total
Robert	16	24	40
Cindy	21	39	60
Jenny	22	28	50
David	37	13	50

2 Record the results in a graph.

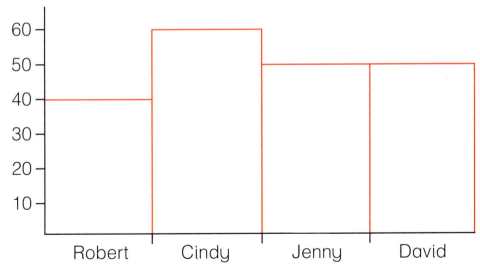

3 Talk about the results.

Cindy jumped 60 meters.

Talk about

 1 Listen and point. Say the words.

Track 27

carry

carry

take

take

climb

climb

run after

run after

umbrella

umbrella

bag

bag

telephone

telephone

fruit

fruit

2 Write the words in exercise 1.

Lesson 1

Vocabulary presentation

Materials: track 27, Activity Resource Book page 15, colored pencils or pens, music

Lesson objectives:	Learn and write the new vocabulary
New vocabulary:	*carry, take, climb, run after, umbrella, bag, telephone, fruit*

Global assessment indicators
a Student works well in teams
b Student presents work with care
c Student respects classroom rules
d Student is interested in learning

1 Bounce into action!
- Say one of the new vocabulary words and act it out or draw it on the board. Have students imitate the word.
- Point and say the words randomly and have students mime the actions.

2 Exercise 1

Listen and point. Say the words.

- Point to the pictures in the book, say *Listen and point* and play track 27.
- Have students point out the pictures as they are mentioned on the track.
- Say *Say the words* and play the track again. Press the pause button after each phrase so students can repeat the words, first together and then individually.

3 Exercise 2

Write the words in exercise 1.

- Ask students to write down the words.
- Go around the room helping and encouraging the students to say the words while they are writing them.

4 Word window (optional activity)
- Ask students to open their Activity Resource Book to page 15.
- Have them write one of the vocabulary words in each section using a black pen or pencil.
- Encourage them to color the umbrella in bright colors.
- Ask them to cut it out along the dotted lines.
- Play music. When the music is playing, students are to walk around the room, find a pair and show them his/her umbrella. When the music stops they must sit down together and take turns saying the new vocabulary words. Play the music again, and repeat the same steps.

5 Bounce on!
1 Divide the class into groups and ask them to sit down in a circle. Hand an object to each group. Play the music. Students are to pass the object from person to person. When the music stops, the student with the object must stand, choose one of the words on the board and perform the corresponding action. The other students are to say the word. Then play the music again and continue playing the game. (5 – 10 minutes)

2 Say the words and have several students come to the front to do the actions and write the words on the board. (5 – 10 minutes)

Multi-ROM task   Student's Multi-ROM

Ask students to complete the Unit 6 Lesson 1 activity on the Student's Multi-ROM to review the vocabulary they have learned.

Interactive presentation. Use the Teacher's Multi-ROM to work with the Student's Book or with the Big Book Builder.

unit 6

Lesson 2
Grammar presentation

Materials: a ball, colored pencils

Lesson objectives: Ask and answer questions using the new vocabulary

Vocabulary review: *carry, take, climb, run after, umbrella, bag, telephone, fruit*

New grammar: *Is he climbing through the window?*
Yes, he is. / No, he isn't.

1 Bounce into action!

- Write the new vocabulary words on the board.
- Ask students to form a circle and give them a ball. They must continue passing the ball until you say *Stop*. The student holding the ball must choose one of the words on the board and do the action.
- The rest of the class is to try to guess the word. Continue in this way with all the words.

2 Exercise 1

Answer the questions.

- Have one of the students come to the front and give him/her two books. Ask *Is he/she carrying two books?* Help the students answer *Yes, he/she is.* Point to the student and ask *Is he/she running after a dog?* Encourage them to answer *No, he/she isn't.* Follow the same steps with the various verbs and objects.
- Write *Today's grammar* on the board and ask students to copy it down.

> **Today's grammar**
> Is he climbing through the window?
> Yes, he is. / No, he isn't.

- Read the questions with the students and ask them to write the answers.

3 Exercise 2

Write the questions for the answers.

- Look at the pictures with the students and ask them to read the answers. Ask them what they think the answer is. Have some of the students come to the front to write down their suggestions and talk about them with the class.
- Ask them to write the questions. Go around the room helping them.

4 Exercise 3

Talk time. Draw Becky Bounce doing something. Ask your friends what she's doing.

- Hand a sheet of paper to each student. Ask them to draw a picture of Becky Bounce doing something.
- Divide the class into pairs. Ask them to take turns showing their pictures and asking and answering questions about the pictures.

5 Bounce on!

1 Spelling activity. Say one of the vocabulary words to a student. The student is to spell the word and then say a sentence using the word. Continue in the same way, making sure that most students have participated in the activity. (5 – 10 minutes)

2 Ask students to write the question below their picture of Becky Bounce. Have several of the students come to the front to show his/her picture and to ask questions about the picture. Encourage the rest of the class to answer. (5 – 10 minutes)

Home Study
page 92

Write the following task instruction on the board and ask students to copy it in the space provided:

"Answer the questions. Circle the correct answer."

Interactive presentation. Use the Teacher's Multi-ROM to work with the Student's Book or with the Big Book Builder.

1 Answer the questions.

1 Is he climbing through the window?

__No, he isn't_____.

2 Is it running after the cat?

__Yes, it is_____.

3 Is she carrying an umbrella?

__No, she isn't_____.

4 Is he taking the fruit from his teacher's desk?

__Yes, he is_____.

2 Write the questions for the answers.

1 __Is she carrying a bag_____?

No, she isn't.

2 __Is he running after the dog_____?

Yes, he is.

3 Draw Becky Bounce doing something.
Ask your friends what she's doing.

Talk time

Is she carrying a chair?

1 Listen and number the sentences in the correct order.

Track 28

Oh, Officer Curtis, now he's running down the street. [3]

There's a bear in Mrs. Dodd's yard. He's climbing through the kitchen window. [1]

And there's Mrs. Dodd. She's running after the bear. Come quickly, Officer Curtis! [4]

And he's taking her umbrella – he's eating it! [2]

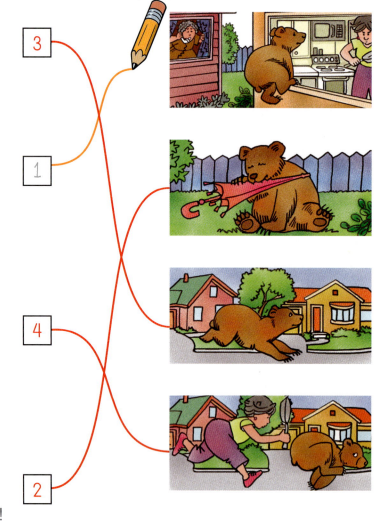

2 Match the sentences to the pictures in exercise 1.

3 Answer the questions.

1 Picture one: Is the bear climbing through the bedroom window?

   No, he isn't_____.

2 Picture three: Is the bear running down the street?

   Yes, he is_____.

unit 6

Read a story

Materials: track 28, colored pencils, sheets of paper for each student, colored pens

Lesson objectives:	Listen to a story, put it in the correct order and answer questions
Vocabulary review:	*climbing, running after, umbrella, taking, carrying*
Grammar review:	*Is he . . . ? Yes, he is. / No, he isn't.*

1 Bounce into action!

- Check that students have completed and understood the task in the Home Study section on page 92. (Answers: p.167)
- Write the vocabulary words on the board.
- Ask the students to read them and close their eyes. Erase one of the words.
- Ask students to open their eyes and guess the missing word. Continue in this way with the rest of the vocabulary.

2 Exercise 1

 Listen and number the sentences in the correct order.

- Tell the students that they are going to listen to a story.
- Look at the pictures with the class and ask them what they think the story will be about.
- Talk about their suggestions.
- Say *Listen and point* and play track 28. Have students point to the pictures as they hear them during the story.
- Read the sentences with the students. Tell them to put the sentences in the correct order by numbering them. Play the track again and encourage the students to order the sentences and write down the numbers.
- Play the track for the third time and press the pause button after each sentence. Check the order of the sentences with the students.

3 Exercise 2

Match the sentences to the pictures in exercise 1.

- Ask students to draw a line from each sentence to the corresponding picture.
- Go around the room correcting their work.

4 Exercise 3

Answer the questions.

- Ask questions to students about the story and encourage them to answer. *Yes, he /she is* or *No, he /she isn't.* Ask *Is the bear taking Mrs. Dodd's umbrella?* Encourage them to answer *Yes, he is.*
- Ask the students to read the questions in the book and have them answer them.
- Go around the room helping them.

5 Bounce on!

1 Ask them what they think happened after Mrs. Dodd ran after the bear. Discuss their suggestions. Encourage them to draw what happened next. Ask them to write a sentence. (10 minutes)

2 Hand out the blank sheets of paper. Ask students to cut the sheet into four pieces. Ask the students what happened first in the story. Write a simple sentence on the board describing what happened first and then ask them to write it on one of the pieces and draw a picture. Do the same thing for what happened next and then at the end. On the remaining part, ask them to write the name of the story. Finally, staple them together to form a story booklet. (15 minutes)

Interactive presentation. Use the Teacher's Multi-ROM to work with the Student's Book or with the Big Book Builder.

T46

Lesson 4

Write about . . . Mr. Rigg and the lion.

Materials: colored pencils, blank sheets of paper

Lesson objectives:	Read and write a story Draw yourself in the story
Vocabulary review:	*carry, take, climb, run after, umbrella, bag, telephone, fruit, jumping, running, walking, holding, laughing*
Grammar review:	*He's jumping through the window.*

1 Bounce into action!

- Write the following words on the board: *carry, take, climb, run after, umbrella, bag, telephone, fruit.*
- Say the words in any order and have students perform the appropriate action.
- Do the action and have students say the word.

2 Exercise 1

Read the story about Mrs. Dodd and the bear.

- Read the story from the previous lesson with the students.
- Ask a few of the students to read the sentences for the whole class.
- Talk about the actions of the bear and Mrs. Dodd.

3 Exercise 2

Write about Mr. Rigg and the lion.

- Tell students they are going to write a story about Mr. Rigg.
- Explain to them that they must read the options and choose the one they prefer.
- Look at the first picture with the students and ask them to read the sentences using the different options. Do the same thing with the other alternatives.
- Ask the students to write their story.
- Go around the room helping them and correcting their work.

4 Exercise 3

Complete the pictures. Draw yourself in the story.

- Ask students to finish the pictures and draw themselves in the story.
- Go around the room encouraging the students and admiring their work.

5 Bounce on!

1 Ask students to draw what happened after Mr. Rigg laughed at the lion or ran after the lion. Ask them to write a sentence below the picture. *The lion is crying. / The lion is climbing a tree.* (10 minutes)

2 Divide the class into groups. Have them take turns showing their pictures and telling their stories. Go around checking that the students are working properly, and help them with their pronunciation. (5 – 10 minutes)

Interactive presentation. Use the Teacher's Multi-ROM to work with the Student's Book or with the Big Book Builder.

Mr. Rigg and the lion.

1 Read the story about Mrs. Dodd and the bear.

2 Write about Mr. Rigg and the lion.

1 There's a lion in Mr. Rigg's yard. He's (jumping / running / walking) _(own answers)_ through the (door / window) _(own answers)_.

2 He's (taking / carrying / holding) _(own answers)_ Mr. Rigg's (umbrella / telephone / bag) _(students' own answers)_.

3 Oh, Officer Brown, now he's running (through the park / down the street / to my house) _(students' own answers)_!

4 There's Mr. Rigg! He's (running after the lion / laughing at the lion) _(students' own answers)_! Come quickly, Officer Brown!

3 Complete the pictures. Draw yourself in the story.

1 Listen and point. Say the words.

Track 29

rescue	help	take care of	fix

examine	drive	answer	operate on

2 Find and circle the words in the puzzle.

```
l  a  f  d  o  u  h  k  a  a
o  p  e  r  a  t  e  o  n  p
p  i  s  e  j  p  l  d  s  f
y  m  b  s  e  g  p  y  w  l
o  m  v  c  h  e  c  k  e  o
f  i  x  u  x  f  l  t  r  x
t  c  h  e  x  a  m  i  n  e
m  l  d  r  i  v  e  k  h  p
t  a  k  e  c  a  r  e  o  f
```

Bounce back

to Unit 5 Write the numbers.

24 _twenty-four_   38 _thirty-eight_   61 _sixty-one_

89 _eighty-nine_   100 _one hundred_

Lesson 5

Vocabulary presentation

Materials: tracks 23 and 29

Lesson objectives: Learn vocabulary about rescues

New vocabulary: *rescue, help, take care of, fix, examine, drive, answer, operate on*

 Bounce into action!

- Divide the class into two groups and sing the song *Free time*, track 23, from unit 5 Lesson 3.
- Encourage students to mime the song's actions.

 Exercise 1

 Listen and point. Say the words.

track 29

- Point to the pictures in the book and say *Listen and point*. Play track 29 and have students point to the pictures.
- Say *Say the words* and play the track. Press the pause button after each word and have them say the words together.

 Exercise 2

Find and circle the words in the puzzle.

- Explain to students that the new vocabulary words are hidden in the puzzle. They must find and circle the words.
- Walk around the room helping the students.
- Have several students come to the front to say the words and show where they are in the puzzle.

 Bounce back. Write the numbers.
(Review activity)

- Say the numbers and have various students come to the front and write them on the board. Say *52* and have the student write *fifty-two*.
- Ask students to say the numbers of the exercise and then write them in their books. Go around the room correcting their work.

 Bounce on!

1 On one side of the board write a few numbers from 1 to 100. On the other side, write the corresponding words but in a different order. Have several students come to the front to say the numbers and draw a line between the numbers and the corresponding words. (5 – 10 minutes)

2 Write the new vocabulary words on the board with the letters jumbled up. Divide the class into groups and have the students put the letters in the correct order and write the words. The first group to write all the words correctly is the winner. (5 – 10 minutes)

 Home Study page 93

Write the following task instructions on the board and ask students to copy them in the space provided:

"Complete the parts of the jigsaw. Write the words."

Multi-ROM task   Student's Multi-ROM

Ask students to complete the Unit 6 Lesson 5 activity on the Student's Multi-ROM to review the vocabulary they have learned.

 **Interactive presentation.** Use the Teacher's Multi-ROM to work with the Student's Book or with the Big Book Builder.

Lesson 6
Grammar and song presentation

Materials: track 30, card, Activity Resource Book page 27, Big Book Builder 2 pages 14 and 15

Lesson objectives: Learn to ask and answer questions using the new vocabulary
Learn the song, *Animal rescue!*

Vocabulary review: *rescue, help, take care of, fix, examine, drive, answer, operate on*

New grammar: *Is he rescuing a bird or a fish? He's rescuing a bird.*

1 Bounce into action!

- Check that students have completed and understood the task in the Home Study section on page 93. (Answers: p.167)
- Divide a card into eight parts and write the vocabulary words on each section. Cut out the words and place them at various places around the room.
- Ask students to read the sentences together.
- Say the words randomly. Students must find the word you said and point to it.

2 Exercise 1

Join the dots and answer the questions.

- Draw a picture of a cat on the board. Have one student come to the front and ask him/her to pretend to take care of the cat. Ask the class *Is he/she taking care of an elephant or a cat?* Help them answer *He's/She's taking care of a cat.* Present the question and answer again, and have students repeat it together.
- Write *Today's grammar* on the board and ask students to copy it down.

> **Today's grammar**
>
> **Is he/she** rescuing a bird or a fish?
>
> **He's / She's** rescuing a bird.

- Read the sentences with the students and ask them to write the answers.

3 Exercise 2

Sing the song: *Animal rescue!*

- Say *Listen* and play track 30.
- Play the track again and encourage students to hum the tune.
- Say the lines of the song one by one and have students repeat them all together.
- Play the track again and sing the song together.
- Ask students to open their Activity Resource Book to page 27 and do the activities.

> **Optional Activity:**
>
> **Big Book Builder 2** pages 14 and 15, *At the Hospital.* Do the activities suggested on pages xi to xix of this book.

4 Bounce on!

1 Divide the class into teams. Write *operate on / owl / iguana* on the board. Each team is to write the question *Is he/she operating on an owl or an iguana?* Each correct answer will be awarded one point. Continue in the same way with the other words. (10 minutes)

2 Ask the students to close their books. Divide the class into groups and ask them to try to remember the lines of the song *Animal rescue!* The team that remembers the whole song correctly wins the game. (5 – 10 minutes)

Home Study page 94

Write the following task instruction on the board and ask students to copy it in the space provided:

"Read the sentences and draw the pictures."

Multi-ROM task   Student's Multi-ROM

Ask the students to listen to the song *Animal rescue!*, track 30, at home until they have memorized it.

Interactive presentation. Use the Teacher's Multi-ROM to work with the Student's Book or with the Big Book Builder.

1 Join the dots and answer the questions.

Today's grammar

Is he rescuing a bird or a fish?
He's rescuing a bird.

2 **3** **4**

1 Is he rescuing a bird or a fish?

He's rescuing a bird_____.

2 Is he driving a car or a truck?

He's driving a truck_____.

3 Is she answering the telephone or an e-mail?

She's answering the telephone_____.

4 Is he examining a cat or a dog?

He's examining a dog_____.

Track 30

Sing the song: Animal rescue!

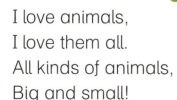

I love animals,
I love them all.
All kinds of animals,
Big and small!

Animal rescue, animal rescue,
That is what I like to do.
Finding them and feeding them,
And taking care of them, too.
Rescuing animals is what I do!

Listen and read. *Jay to the rescue!*

Track 31

1

Mom: What's Jay doing?
Sandy: He's climbing Mr. Trent's apple tree.
Mom: Is he eating the apples?
Sandy: I don't know.

2

Mom: Is he making a tree house?
Sandy: I don't know.

3

Mom: Is he fixing the swing?
Sandy: I don't know.

4

Mom: Oh, look! He's rescuing a small cat.
Sandy: It's Tabatha! It's Mr. Trent's cat.

2 **Write a sentence about what you think Mr. Trent is doing.**

I think Mr. Trent is _(students' own answers)_____.

unit 6

Lesson 7
Read a story

Materials: tracks 30 and 31, 5 photocopies of the story, Big Book Builder 2 pages 14 and 15

Lesson objectives:	Listen to a story
Grammar review:	*Is he . . . ?*

 Bounce into action!

- Check that students have completed and understood the task in the Home Study section on page 94. (Answers: p.167)
- Get students to sing *Animal rescue!* Play track 30 to help them remember the song.
- Divide the class into three groups and get each group to sing one verse of the song.

 Exercise 1

 Listen and read. *Jay to the rescue!*

- Look at the pictures with the students and tell them that they are going to listen to a story.
- Ask them to say what they think the story will be about.
- Discuss their suggestions and write a few down on the board.
- Say *Listen* and play track 31. Encourage the students to point to the pictures as they hear them during the story.
- Ask them to say what they think the story is about. Point to their suggestions on the board and talk about the similarities to the story they have just heard.
- Talk about the actions of Jay.
- Read the story with the students. Ask a few students to read the sentences for the whole class.

 Exercise 2

Write a sentence about what you think Mr. Trent is doing.

- Ask them what they think Mr. Trent is doing while Jay is trying to rescue the cat.
- Discuss their suggestions.
- Ask them to write a sentence in their books about what they think Mr. Trent is doing.
- While they are working, go around the room correcting the sentences.

> **Optional Activity:**
> **Big Book Builder 2** pages 14 and 15, *At the Hospital.* Do the activities suggested on pages xi to xix of this book.

 Bounce on!

1 Cut up the photocopies of the story. Divide the class into five groups and check that each group has the whole story. Ask them to put the story in the correct order. (5 – 10 minutes)

2 Divide the class into two teams. Ask one member from each team to come to the front. Say something from the story (either true or false). If it is false, the children are to write *F* on the board, if it is true they are to write *T*. The team that writes the correct answer first wins a point. At the end of the game, the team with the most points is the winner. (15 minutes)

> **Multi-ROM task**   Student's Multi-ROM
>
> Ask the students to listen to the story *Jay to the rescue!*, track 31, at home until they can perform a role-play during the next class.

> **Interactive presentation.** Use the Teacher's Multi-ROM to work with the Student's Book or with the Big Book Builder.

Lesson 8

Bounce around: Language

Materials: track 31, Assessment Pack pages 4, 5 and 29

Lesson objectives: Talk about the importance of taking care of animals
Practice the vocabulary learned

Vocabulary review: *animals, rescue, help, take care of, examine, operate on*

① Bounce into action!

- Ask students to come to the front to role-play the story *Jay to the rescue!* in pairs. Play track 31 if necessary.

② Exercise 1

Read the poster and answer the questions.

- Look at pictures with the students and read the contents of the poster together.
- Ask the students which one of them has a pet, and talk about their animals and the importance of looking after them, loving them and caring for them when they are sick.
- Answer the questions.

③ Exercise 2

 Talk about animal care. Color the correct face.

- Ask them where they think children or adults should take an animal that is sick and who looks after them.
- Ask the children to tell you what people who work in animal hospitals do. Help them use the vocabulary learned during the unit.

④ Bounce on!

1 Divide the class into groups. Students must work in teams to write sentences about the book's poster. The team to write the most correct sentences wins. (10 minutes)

2 Say sentences about the care animals need. If the sentences you say are correct, then students are to stand up. If what you are saying is incorrect, students are to correct the sentence. (5 – 10 minutes)

Language Assessment: Photocopy the language assessment sheet on page 29 of the Assessment Pack. Give each student a copy to complete in order to check what they have learned over the course of the unit.

 Self Assessment: Photocopy the self assessment sheet on page 4 of the Assessment Pack. Give a copy to each student for them to complete on their own. Offer help where necessary.

Global Assessment: Complete the global assessment on page 5 of the Assessment Pack. Check whether the objectives set out at the start of the unit were achieved by your students. Keep a record to refer back to in coming units.

Interactive presentation. Use the Teacher's Multi-ROM to work with the Student's Book or with the Big Book Builder.

Bounce around: Language

 1 Read the poster and answer the questions.

a. PetCare is the name of:
   1) the hospital
   2) the doctor

b. The hospital is for:
   1) people
   2) animals

c. The hospital closes at:
   1) 9.00
   2) 6.00

d. 241-9633 is the:
   1) telephone number
   2) the time the hospital opens

PetCare Hospital

Vet: Dr. P. Wang

2246 Overton Drive, Hattsville
Tel: 241-9633
9.00am - 6.00pm

 2 Talk about animal care. Color the correct face.

It's important to take care of animals.

 I agree.

 I don't agree.

unit 7

LESSON 1

 1 Listen and point. Say the words.

Track 32

pizza

pizza

hamburger

hamburger

milk

milk

lemonade

lemonade

french fries

french fries

Jello

Jello

salad

salad

apple pie

apple pie

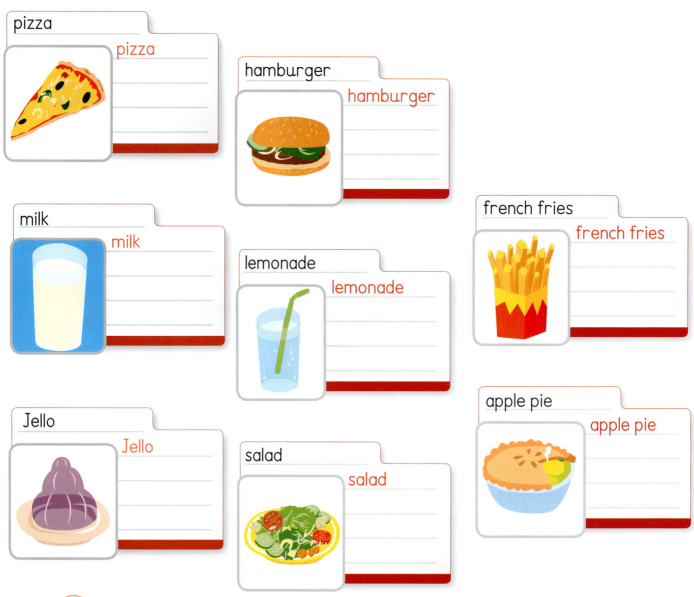

2 Write the words in exercise 1.

unit 7

Lesson 1

Vocabulary presentation

Materials: track 32, Activity Resource Book page 17, pictures of the new vocabulary, colored pencils, glue

Lesson objectives:	Learn vocabulary about food
New vocabulary:	*pizza, hamburger, french fries, milk, lemonade, apple pie, jello, salad*

Global assessment indicators

a Student works well in teams
b Student presents work with care
c Student respects classroom rules
d Student is interested in learning

1 Bounce into action!

- Draw your favorite food on the board and talk about it with the students. Ask them about their favorite food.
- Explain to them that you are going to talk about food and elicit any words they already know relating to food.
- Write the word *Food* in the center of the board and write all the students' suggestions around it.

2 Exercise 1

Listen and point. Say the words.

- Say *Listen and point* and play track 32.
- Have students point out the pictures as they are mentioned on the track.
- Say *Say the words* and play the track again. Press the pause button after each word so students can repeat them together.

3 Exercise 2

Write the words in exercise 1.

- Ask students to write down the words.
- Go around the room helping and encouraging the students to say the words while they are writing them.

4 Word window (optional activity)

- Ask students to open their Activity Resource Book to page 17. Ask them to color in and cut out the pictures of food, making sure they do not cut the labels. Have them write the corresponding words with a pen.
- Show them how to fold the labels and place the food on the drawing of a table.
- Ask students to stand up and walk around the room. Play music. When the music stops, they are to sit next to the nearest person and take turns showing and saying the food names.

5 Bounce on!

1   Place the pictures of the new vocabulary on the board. Ask one of the students to come to the front. Ask them to write the name of the food that you say below the correct picture. Then ask him/her to make a sentence with the word. Repeat the activity by having other students come to the front. (5 – 10 minutes)

2 Write the food words on the board and have students say the food. Ask them to close their eyes. Erase one of the words and encourage them to name the missing word. Repeat the same steps with other words. (5 – 10 minutes)

Home Study page 95

Write the following task instructions on the board and ask students to copy them in the space provided:

"Complete the puzzle. Write the words in the correct category."

Multi-ROM task   Student's Multi-ROM

Ask students to complete the Unit 7 Lesson 1 activity on the Student's Multi-ROM to review the vocabulary they have learned.

Interactive presentation. Use the Teacher's Multi-ROM to work with the Student's Book or with the Big Book Builder.

T52

unit 7

Lesson 2
Grammar presentation

Lesson objectives:	Ask and answer questions about food
Vocabulary review:	Food
New grammar:	*Are they eating apple pie?* *Yes, they are. / No, they aren't.*

1 Bounce into action!
- Check that students have completed and understood the task in the Home Study section on page 95. (Answers: p.167).
- Draw one of the items of food on the board in stages. Encourage students to try to guess what it is and say it while you are drawing it. When they have guessed the word correctly draw another item of food. Continue in this way with all the words.
- Point to the pictures randomly and have students say them together and individually.

2 Exercise 1

Unscramble the words and answer the questions.

- Write the word *pizza* on the board. Have two students come to the front and ask them to pretend to be eating pizza. Ask the rest of the class *Are they drinking lemonade?* Help them to answer *No, they aren't*. Ask *Are they eating pizza?* Help the rest of the class to answer *Yes, they are*. Model the new structure again and have students repeat the sentences together several times.
- Write *Today's grammar* on the board and ask students to copy it down.

Today's grammar

Are they	eating apple pie?
	drinking milk?

Yes, they are. / No, they aren't.

- Read the questions with the students and explain that the food words are jumbled up. Have them answer the question orally, and then have a student come to the front to write the first word; get someone else to answer the question.
- Ask them to finish the exercise on their own.
- While they are working, go around the room helping them.

3 Exercise 2

Write the questions for the answers.

- Look at the pictures with the students and ask a few of them to read the answers for the class. Ask them what they think is the correct question for the first answer.
- Ask them to write the questions in their books. Go around the room correcting their work.

Optional Activity:

Big Book Builder 2 pages 16 and 17, *At the Restaurant*. Do the activities suggested on pages xi to xix of this book.

---

4 Bounce on!

1 Divide the group into two teams. Ask a member from each team to come to the front. Say *Pizza* and have the students write the word correctly on the board. The first student to write it correctly wins a point. The team with the most points wins the game. (5 minutes)

2 Play *Hangman*. Divide the class into two teams. Have students from each team come to the front and draw a dash for each of the letters in the word they are thinking about. The other team says letters of the alphabet to try to guess the words. (5 – 10 minutes)

Interactive presentation. Use the Teacher's Multi-ROM to work with the Student's Book or with the Big Book Builder.

1 Unscramble the words and answer the questions.

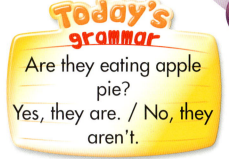
Today's grammar
Are they eating apple pie?
Yes, they are. / No, they aren't.

 1  2  3  4

1 Are they eating a p p l e p i e ?

Yes, _they are_ .

2 Are they making J e l l o ?

No, they aren't .

3 Are they drinking l e m o n a d e ?

Yes, they are .

4 Are they eating h a m b u r g e r s ?

Yes, they are .

2 Write the questions for the answers.

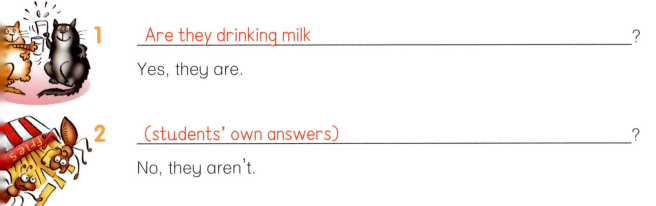

1 _Are they drinking milk_ ?

Yes, they are.

2 _(students' own answers)_ ?

No, they aren't.

1 Read and draw.

Anna   Daniel

Ben
Deb

Tessa   Maggie

1 Look at Anna and Daniel.

Are they drinking milk?   No, they aren't.

Are they drinking lemonade?   Yes, they are.

2 Look at Ben and Deb.

Are they buying hamburgers?   Yes, they are.

3 Look at Tessa and Maggie.

Are they making salad?   No, they aren't.

Are they making jello?   Yes, they are.

2 Draw what Dan and Dave
are eating. Ask your friends. (students' own answers)

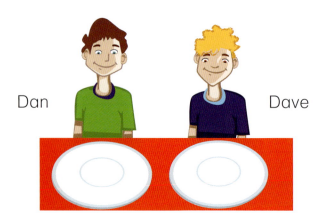

Dan   Dave

Talk time

Are they
eating salad?

unit 7

Lesson 3
Reading practice

Materials: colored pencils, blank sheets of paper for each student, Big Book Builder 2 pages 16 and 17

Lesson objectives:	Read about food
	Ask and answer questions about food
Vocabulary review:	Food
Grammar review:	*Are they . . . Yes, they are. / No, they aren't.*

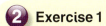 Bounce into action!

- Have two of the students come to the front and say *Jello* to them. They must write the word on the board and then pretend to eat it.
- Ask the rest of the class *Are they drinking milk?* The students must reply together *No, they aren't.* Ask *Are they eating jello?* Encourage them to answer *Yes, they are.*
- Have two other students come to the front and follow the same procedure with the rest of the food words.

② Exercise 1

Read and draw.

- Look at the pictures and read the question and answers with the students.
- Ask a few students to read the sentences for the whole class.
- Ask them to read the sentences again on their own and draw a picture of the corresponding food.
- Go around the room helping and encouraging the students.

> **Optional Activity:**
> **Big Book Builder 2** pages 16 and 17, *At the Restaurant.* Do the activities suggested on pages xi to xix of this book.

Exercise 2

Talk time. Draw what Dan and Dave are eating. Ask your friends.

- Explain to students that they have to draw what Dan and Dave are eating. Go around the room encouraging them to say the name of the food they are drawing.
- Have a few students come to the front to show their pictures. Ask them *Are they eating …?* Encourage them to answer *Yes, they are* or *No, they aren't,* as appropriate.
- Divide the class into pairs. Explain to them that they are to take it in turns to show their picture and ask and answer questions about Dan and Dave's food.
- Go around the room helping them with their pronunciation.

Bounce on!

1 Give a sheet of paper to each student. Tell them to draw a picture and write the name of their favorite food. Ask a few students to come to the front and say the name of their favorite food and give their reasons why. Display the pictures around the room. (10 – 15 minutes)

2 Ask students to write two questions and answers about the food of Dan and Dave: *Are they eating apple pie? / No, they aren't. / Are they eating salad? / Yes, they are.* (5 – 10 minutes)

Home Study page 96

Write the following task instructions on the board and ask students to copy them in the space provided:

"Decipher the secret message. Answer the question. Write a new message to share with your group during the next class."

Interactive presentation. Use the Teacher's Multi-ROM to work with the Student's Book or with the Big Book Builder.

unit 7

Lesson 4

Write about . . . making things.

Materials: cards or sheets of paper, colored pencils, Big Book Builder 2 pages 16 and 17

Lesson objectives:	Read a text
	Write a story about the food Kelly and Ken are making
Vocabulary review:	Food

1 Bounce into action!

- Check that students have completed and understood the task in the Home Study section on page 96. (Answers: p. 168)
- Write the food words on cards or sheets of paper and place them at various points around the room and get the students to stand up.
- Say one of the words. Students near the word are to point to it, do the action and then sit down.
- Continue in the same way until all the words have been identified and all the students have returned to their seats.

2 Exercise 1

Read about what Kelly and Ken are making.

- Read the text with the students.
- Talk about the actions of the koalas.
- Ask comprehension questions to check the students have understood.

3 Exercise 2

Write about the different food Kelly and Ken are making. Use one of the choices below.

- Tell students that Kelly and Ken are making more food.
- Explain that they must write about what they are making.

- Ask the students to read the two choices. Encourage them to choose the option they like better.
- Have several students come to the front and write the first sentence using each of the two choices: *Kelly and Ken are in the kitchen at Ken's house making jello. / Kelly and Ken are in the kitchen at Ken's house making an apple pie.*
- Have students write the rest of the text on their own.
- While they are working, go around the room helping them and correcting their work.

Optional Activity:

Big Book Builder 2 pages 16 and 17, *At the Restaurant.* Do the activities suggested on pages xi to xix of this book.

4 Bounce on!

1 Ask students to draw a picture of Ken and Kelly making the food they described. They are to draw a large *jello* and color it yellow and orange. If they choose the other option, they are to draw the picture of a large apple pie with red and green apples. (5 – 10 minutes)

2 Divide the class into pairs. Ask them to take turns showing their drawing to their partner and telling the story aloud. Go around helping the pairs with their pronunciation. (10 minutes)

Interactive presentation. Use the Teacher's Multi-ROM to work with the Student's Book or with the Big Book Builder.

 **making things.**

1 Read about what Kelly and Ken are making.

Kelly and Ken are in the kitchen at Ken's house making a pizza.

They're making a big ham and cheese pizza for a lot of people. Yummy!

Delicious! It's Kelly's birthday and they're calling all their friends.

"Come to the pizza party," says Kelly. "Great!" say their friends.

2 Write about the different food Kelly and Ken are making. Use one of the choices below.

Jello big lemon and orange	an apple pie big red and green

Kelly and Ken are __(students' own answers)_____

_____

_____

_____

_____

_____.

1 Listen and point. Say the words.

Track 33

set the table 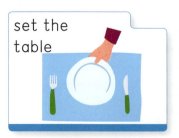	wash the dishes 	pour the drinks 	serve the food 

brownies 	potato chips 	soda 	sausages 

 2 Look at the pictures. Write sentences.

1 He's _setting the table_ .

2 He's _washing the dishes_ .

3 He's _pouring the drinks_ .

4 He's _serving the food_ .

3 Answer the questions.

1 It's brown and square. What is it?   _a brownie_ .

2 It's round and yellow. What is it?   _a potato chip_ .

Lesson 5

Vocabulary presentation

Materials: tracks 23 and 33

Lesson objectives:	Learn more vocabulary about food
New vocabulary:	*set the table, wash the dishes, pour the drinks, serve the food, brownies, potato chips, soda, sausages*

1 Bounce into action!

- Play track 23. Sing the song *Free time* from unit 5 Lesson 3.
- Get students to mime the song's actions as they are singing the song.

2 Exercise 1

Listen and point. Say the words.

- Point to the pictures in the book and say *Listen and point.* Play track 33. Get students to point to the pictures as they are mentioned on the track.
- Say *Say the words.* Play the track again and stop it after each word so students can repeat the words together, then individually.

3 Exercise 2

Look at the pictures. Write sentences.

- Get some of the students to read the activities for the whole class. Ask them to look at the pictures and ask them to say what activities people normally do first. Encourage them to number the activities in a chronological order.

- Get one of the students to come to the front and ask him / her to write the first sentence: *He's setting the table.*
- Get the students to write the rest of the sentences in their books.
- Go around the room correcting their work.

4 Exercise 3

Answer the questions.

- Read the riddles with the students and encourage them to guess the words.
- Ask them to write the answers.
- Go around the room helping and encouraging the students.

5 Bounce on!

1 Explain to the students that you are going to say sentences. If the sentence starts with *Bounce says*, they must do the action. If you don't say *Bounce says*, they must remain still. Say *Wash the dishes.* Students must remain still. Say *Bounce says eat potato chips.* Students must pretend to eat potato chips. (5 – 10 minutes)

2 Get several students to come to the front and whisper one of the phrases or words from the vocabulary to them. They must perform the corresponding actions while the class tries to guess the word or phrases. (5 – 10 minutes)

Multi-ROM task   Student's Multi-ROM

Ask students to complete the Unit 7 Lesson 5 activity on the Student's Multi-ROM to review the vocabulary they have learned.

Interactive presentation. Use the Teacher's Multi-ROM to work with the Student's Book or with the Big Book Builder.

unit 7

Lesson 6

Grammar presentation

Materials: music, drawing of a pizza, sausages, potato chips, a soft drink and some brownies

Lesson objectives:	Learn to ask and answer questions about food
Vocabulary review:	All the words associated with food
New grammar:	*Are the girls eating hamburgers or pizza?*

1 Bounce into action!

- Explain to the students that you are going to say the new vocabulary words and phrases while playing music. While the music is playing they must do the correct action. When the music stops they must not move.
- Any student moving out of turn, or doing the wrong action, is out of the game.

2 Exercise 1

Look at the picture and answer the questions.

- Ask a group of students to come to the front and hand them the picture of the sausages. Ask them to pretend to eat them. Point to their actions and ask *Are they eating sausages or pizza?* Encourage the students to answer *Sausages.* Repeat the question and get the class to say the new structure again together.
- Get other students to come to the front and follow the same steps with the other pictures.
- Write *Today's grammar* on the board and ask students to copy it down.

> **Today's grammar**
> Are the girls eating sausages or pizza?
> Are the boys drinking soda or milk?

- Read the exercise's first question with the students and encourage them to answer. Get one of the students to come to the front to write the word indicated. Ask them to read and answer the other questions on their own.
- Go around the room correcting the answers.

3 Bounce back. Unscramble the questions. (Review activity)

- Explain to students that the words of the questions are all jumbled up and that they must put them in the correct order and write them out correctly, as well as answering them.
- Ask a few students to put the question in the correct order.
- Get one of the students to come to the front to write the first question.
- Get the other students to answer it.
- Ask them to complete the rest of the exercise on their own.

4 Bounce on!

1 Explain to the class that they are going to pretend to be hungry little squirrels looking at people eating in a restaurant. Divide the class into pairs and encourage them to think about words for food and create a dialogue: *Are the girls eating sausages or chips? / Chips. / Are they drinking milk or soda? / Soda. / Oh! I'm hungry!* (10 minutes)

2 Ask the class to sit in a circle. Say *Bounce is setting the table.* The next student is to repeat the sentence and add another phrase: *Bounce is setting the table and making apple pie.* Continue in this way until you have created a chain of five or six phrases, and then start another round. (5 – 10 minutes)

Home Study page 97

Write the following task instructions on the board and ask students to copy them in the space provided:

"Put the words in the correct order to form questions. Write the answers."

Interactive presentation. Use the Teacher's Multi-ROM to work with the Student's Book or with the Big Book Builder.

Look at the picture and answer the questions.

Today's grammar

Are the girls eating hamburgers or pizza?

1 Are the girls eating hamburgers or pizza?

They're eating pizza   .

2 Are the boys drinking soda or milk?

They're drinking soda   .

3 Are Mom and Dad setting the table or washing the dishes?

They're washing the dishes   .

4 Are Grandpa and Grandma making apple pie or Jello?

They're making apple pie   .

Bounce back

to Unit 6 Unscramble the questions.

1 making pizza he a Is?

Is he making a pizza?   .

2 she bird Is rescuing a?

Is she rescuing a bird?   .

3 an he Is e-mail answering?

Is he answering an e-mail?   .

Sing the song: The Jello men

Look at the Jello men,
Going wobble, wobble, wobble.
They're in the kitchen,
Going gobble, gobble, gobble.

Are they eating apple pie?
Are they eating cake?
Are they eating sausages?
Now that's a big mistake.

Are they eating pizza now?
Are they eating chips?
No, look, they're eating caramels.
They're sticking to their lips.

2 Track 35 Listen again and draw the food words in exercise 1.

unit 7

Lesson 7

Song presentation

Materials: tracks 34 and 35, colored pencils, Activity Resource Book page 28

Lesson objectives:	Learn the song *The Jello men*
Vocabulary review:	Food
Grammar review:	*Are they eating . . . ?*

1 Bounce into action!

- Check that students have completed and understood the task in the Home Study section on page 97. (Answers: p. 168)
- Divide the class into pairs. Write the number *5* on the board.
- Ask the pairs *Are the children drinking lemonade or milk?*
- One of the students should place their hand on the table and say *Lemonade*; his/her partner then places their hand over their partner's hand and says *Milk*. The first student then places their other hand above their partner's, and says *Lemonade* again. They must put their hands on top of each other alternately and repeat the words five times. The word that falls in the fifth position is the correct answer.
- Write another number on the board and ask another question.

2 Exercise 1

track 34

Sing the song: *The Jello men.*

- Tell students they are going to listen to a song. Say *Listen* and play track 34.
- Play the track again and encourage students to sing the words *gobble, gobble, gobble.*
- Model the lines of the song and get students to repeat the lines all together.
- Play the track again and sing the song together.
- Ask students to open their Activity Resource Book to page 28 and do the activities.

3 Exercise 2

track 35

Listen again and draw the food words in exercise 1.

- Explain to students that they are going to complete the missing food words.
- Play track 35 and press the pause button after each verse to allow students to draw the words.
- Play the track again and correct the work with the students.

4 Bounce on!

1 Ask students to draw the Jello men in the kitchen with all the food they are eating. (10 minutes)

2 Ask students to write a sentence below their pictures, for example, *The Jello men are eating caramels.* (5 – 10 minutes)

Multi-ROM task Student's Multi-ROM	 **Interactive presentation.** Use the Teacher's Multi-ROM to work with the Student's Book or with the Big Book Builder.
Ask the students to listen to the song *The Jello men*, track 34, at home until they have memorized it.	**T58**

Lesson 8

Bounce around: Natural Science

Materials: track 34, sheets of paper for each student, colored pencils, pictures of food, Assessment Pack pages 4, 5 and 30

Lesson objectives:	Learn through natural science Practice the unit's language
Vocabulary review:	Food

 Bounce into action!

- Play track 34. Sing the song *The Jello men*. Divide the class into as many groups as there are verses in the song.
- Point to the groups in turn and sing the song.
- Point to the groups randomly and sing the song in any order.

 Exercise 1

Put the foods into the correct category.

- Place pictures of food around the class. Write the words *Food* and *Beverages* on the board. Ask a student to take the picture of the food you are saying. Then ask them to place the picture on the board in the correct category. Continue with all the food words and place them in the correct category. Ask the students to think about another way of classifying the pictures and classify them accordingly.
- Do the activity in the book and place the food in the correct category.
- Check that the students are doing the exercise correctly.

Exercise 2

Talk about food.

- Say *Let's talk about food*. Ask students about their favorite food. Help them answer using the grammatical structure *I like…*
- Encourage students to use the vocabulary they have learned during the unit. Then talk about their food dislikes using the grammatical structure *I don't like*.

 **Bounce on!**

1 Hand out sheets of paper to each student and ask them to draw nine squares. Ask them to write a food word in each square. Play *Bingo!* using the food words and pictures. Each time you say a food word that is in one of their squares, they are to check (✓) the square. The first student to check all the nine squares calls out *Bingo!* and is the winner.

2 Hand a sheet of paper to each student. Say *Draw a big plate*. Encourage them to draw their favorite food taking into account the various categories, according to those in the book. (10 minutes)

Language Assessment: Photocopy the language assessment sheet on page 30 of the Assessment Pack. Give each student a copy to complete in order to check what they have learned over the course of the unit.

 Self Assessment: Photocopy the self assessment sheet on page 4 of the Assessment Pack. Give a copy to each student for them to complete on their own. Offer help where necessary.

Global Assessment: Complete the global assessment on page 5 of the Assessment Pack. Check whether the objectives set out at the start of the unit were achieved by your students. Keep a record to refer back to in coming units.

Interactive presentation. Use the Teacher's Multi-ROM to work with the Student's Book or with the Big Book Builder.

Bounce around: Natural Science

1 Put the foods into the correct category.

eggs

rice

sausage

orange

fish

carrots

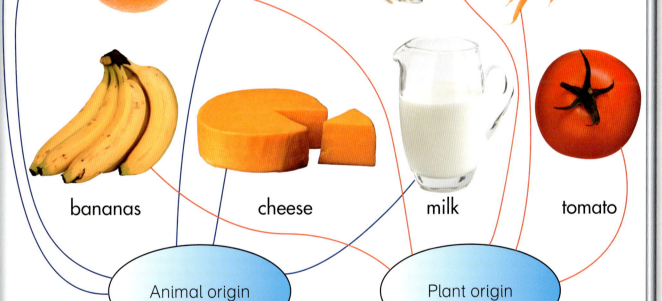

bananas

cheese

milk

tomato

Animal origin

Plant origin

2 Talk about food.

I like bananas.

Talk about

unit
8

LESSON
1

 1 Listen and point. Say the words.

Track 36

poster

poster

invitation

invitation

band

band

prepare

prepare

decorations

decorations

practice

practice

design

design

decorate

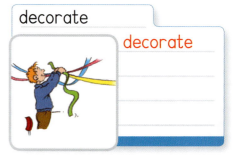

decorate

 2 Write the words in exercise 1.

Lesson 1

Vocabulary presentation

Materials: track 36, cards, colored crepe or tissue paper, glue, colored pencils or pens, glitter glue

Lesson objectives: Learn vocabulary about preparing for parties

New vocabulary: *poster, invitation, decorations, band, prepare, decorate, practice, design*

Global assessment indicators

a Student works well in teams
b Student presents work with care
c Student respects classroom rules
d Student is interested in learning

1 Bounce into action!

- Say *I love parties!* Explain to students that you are going to talk about parties. Discuss the preparations, food, decorations, gifts, etc.
- Elicit from students all the words they know relating to parties.
- Write the word *Party* on the board and write all of the students' suggestions around it.

2 Exercise 1

Listen and point. Say the words.

- Point to the pictures, say *Listen and point* and play track 36.
- Have students point out the pictures as they are mentioned on the track.
- Say *Say the words* and play the track again. Press the pause button after each word so students can repeat them together.

3 Exercise 2

Write the words in exercise 1.

- Ask students to write down the words.
- Go around the room helping and encouraging the students to say the words while they are writing them.

4 Word window (optional activity)

- Divide the class into four groups. Give some cards to each of the groups. Ask them to design a poster for a school party using the new vocabulary words.
- Encourage them to decorate their posters using colored pencils and pens and crepe or tissue paper and glitter glue.
- Have some of the students come to the front to show their posters and say the new words. Display the posters around the room.

5 Bounce on!

1 Write the vocabulary words on the board. Ask students to memorize them. Have them close their eyes. Erase one of the words and ask them to identify the missing word. The student who guesses the word first takes your place at the board and repeats the exercise. (10 minutes)

2 Write the new words with all the letters jumbled up. In groups, ask the students to put the letters in the correct order and write the words. The first group to complete all the words correctly wins. (10 minutes)

Multi-ROM task Student's Multi-ROM

Ask students to complete the Unit 8 Lesson 1 activity on the Student's Multi-ROM to review the vocabulary they have learned.

Interactive presentation. Use the Teacher's Multi-ROM to work with the Student's Book or with the Big Book Builder.

unit 8

Lesson 2

Grammar and song presentation

Materials: track 37, sheets of paper with the new words, Activity Resource Book page 29

Lesson objectives: Ask about preparations for a party
Learn the song *Party preparations*.

New grammar: *Are you designing the posters?*
Yes, I am. / No, I'm not.

1 Bounce into action!

- Write the words of the new vocabulary and place them around the classroom. Ask students to read the words all together.
- Say the words randomly and get students to point to them.
- Change the order and speed at which you say the words.

2 Exercise 1

Answer the questions.

- Ask a student to pretend to be preparing for a party. Ask *Are you writing the invitation?* and get them to answer *Yes, I am* or *No, I'm not*. Repeat the structure with other students. Ask them to read the questions in the book and answer them.
- Write *Today's grammar* on the board and ask students to copy it down.

> **Today's grammar**
>
> Are you designing the posters?
> Yes, I am. / No, I'm not.

3 Exercise 2

 ### Sing the song: *Party preparations*

- Tell students they are going to listen to a song. Say *Listen* and play track 37.
- Model each line in the song and have students repeat the lines together.
- Play the song again and sing it together.
- Ask students to open their Activity Resource Book to page 29 and do the activities.

4 Bounce on!

1 Divide the class into groups. Ask them to pretend that they are preparing for a party. Each student should choose an activity and do the corresponding mime. Have the different groups come to the front and encourage the rest of the students to ask *Are you decorating the room?* The students doing the mime answer *Yes, I am* or *No, I'm not*. (10 minutes)

2 Write the song on the board; however, do not write the words *party, preparing, fun, designing, invitations, food,* or *celebrations*. Divide the class into pairs. Play the track again and have students complete the missing words. Play the track again and check the work with the students. (10 minutes)

 Home Study page 98

Write the following task instructions on the board and ask students to copy them in the space provided:

"Read the invitation and answer the questions. Draw your costume for the party."

Multi-ROM task Student's Multi-ROM

Ask the students to listen to the song *Party preparations*, track 37, at home until they have memorized it.

 **Interactive presentation.** Use the Teacher's Multi-ROM to work with the Student's Book or with the Big Book Builder.

 Answer the questions.

Today's grammar

Are you designing the posters?
Yes, I am. / No, I'm not.

1 Rudy: Are you designing the posters?

Rick: Yes, <u>I am</u>.

2 Rudy: Are you making the decorations?

Marnie: <u>No, I'm not</u>.

Rudy: What are you doing?

Marnie: I'm writing invitations.

3 Rudy: Are you practicing for the party?

Katie: <u>Yes, I am</u>.

Track 37

Sing the song: Party preparations

Party preparations,
So much to be done!
Party preparations,
They're a lot of fun!

Designing party posters,
Writing invitations.
Preparing lots of party food,
For our celebration!

1 Imagine you are preparing for your party.
Answer the questions for you.
Use *Yes, I am* and *No, I'm not.*

1 Are you designing a poster?

(students' own answers)

2 Are you preparing the food?

(students' own answers)

3 Are you decorating the room?

(students' own answers)

4 Are you writing the invitations?

(students' own answers)

2 Draw pictures of your party preparations from exercise 1.

(students' own answers)

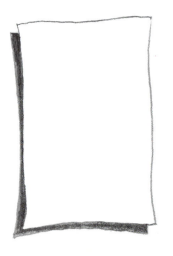

3 Ask your friends what they are doing.
Tell them about your activity.

Talk time

Are you designing a poster? Yes, I am.

Lesson 3

Consolidation

Materials: track 37, Big Book Builder 2 pages 18 and 19

Lesson objectives:	Read and answer questions
	Discuss preparations for parties
Vocabulary review:	Preparations for a party
Grammar review:	*Are you . . . ? Yes, I am / No, I'm not.*

 Bounce into action!

- Check that students have completed and understood the task in the Home Study section on page 98. (Answers: p.168)
- Play track 37. Sing the song *Party preparations*.
- Divide the class into four groups. Each group should sing two lines of the song.
- One by one, point to the groups and sing the song.
- Point to the groups randomly and sing the song in any order.

 Exercise 1

Imagine you are preparing for your party. Answer the questions for you. Use *Yes, I am* and *No, I'm not.*

- Explain to students that they are going to pretend to be preparing for their party. Explain that they need to choose which activities they are going to be doing (i.e. designing the poster, preparing the food, decorating the room or writing the invitations).
- Read the first question and encourage the students who have chosen that particular activity to answer the question by saying *Yes, I am.* The others are to answer *No, I'm not.*
- Ask students to answer the questions in their books. Go around the room helping them.

Exercise 2

Draw pictures of your party preparations from exercise 1.

- Ask students to complete the pictures of the party preparations they have chosen.
- Go around admiring the students' work and encouraging them to say the activities they have chosen.

 Exercise 3

Talk time. Ask your friends what they are doing. Tell them about your activity.

- Divide the students into pairs. They must take turns asking and answering questions about the activities they have chosen. *What are you doing? I'm decorating the room.*
- Go around helping the pairs with their pronunciation.

> **Optional Activity:**
>
> **Big Book Builder 2** pages 18 and 19, *The Concert*. Do the activities suggested on pages xi to xix of this book.

 Bounce on!

1 Ask students to write a sentence about the activities they have chosen: *I'm preparing the food.* (5 minutes)

2 Have one of the students write his/her sentence on the board with the words jumbled up. Ask another student to put it in the correct order. Continue in this way with several students. Correct the spelling.

 Home Study page 99
Write the following task instructions on the board and ask students to copy them in the space provided:

"Draw yourself and two friends. Choose one of the tasks in the box and write the letter under each picture. Answer the questions."

Interactive presentation. Use the Teacher's Multi-ROM to work with the Student's Book or with the Big Book Builder.

unit 8

Lesson 4

Write about . . . what people are doing.

Materials: a sheet of paper for each student, a ball, Big Book Builder 2 pages 18 and 19

Lesson objectives:	Write an e-mail invitation
Vocabulary review:	Party preparations

1 Bounce into action!

- Check that students have completed and understood the task in the Home Study section on page 99. (Answers: p.168)
- Write the new vocabulary words on the board. One by one, point to the words and ask students to say them all together. Erase the words.
- Hand a sheet of paper to each student. Ask students to write down all the words they remember.
- Have some of the students come to the front and write the words for the whole class.

2 Exercise 1

Read the e-mail invitation to Kathy.

- Read Kathy's invitation with the students. Ask a few to read the sentences for the whole class.
- Ask comprehension questions to the students about the activities to check they have understood. Ask, for example, *What is Jack doing? / What is Fred doing? / What is Angela doing? / What is Lucy doing?*

3 Exercise 2

Write an e-mail invitation to a friend for your birthday.

- Explain to students that they are going to write an e-mail to a friend to invite him/her to a party.
- On the board, write an invitation with the class to be used as a model. Encourage students to suggest the sentences.
- Read the invitation they have just written.
- Ask students to write a similar invitation to a friend. Go around helping them formulate their ideas and write the sentences.

> **Optional Activity:**
> **Big Book Builder 2** pages 18 and 19, *The Concert*. Do the activities suggested on pages xi to xix of this book.

4 Bounce on!

1 Ask students to think about what they would like to do when preparing a party. Throw a ball to a student and ask *Are you making pizza?* They are to answer *Yes, I am* or *No, I'm not. I'm …* Continue asking several students. Then form pairs and have the students ask each other what they are doing. Go around the tables listening to them and correcting their pronunciation. (10 minutes)

2 Ask students to read Kathy's invitation again. Tell them that you are going to say sentences. If you say something that is incorrect, they are to raise their hands and correct it. If what you are saying is correct, they must not say anything. Say *Fred is making pizza*. Students must raise their hands and say *No! Fred is decorating the room!* Say *Jack is designing posters*. The students must remain silent. (5 minutes)

> **Interactive presentation.** Use the Teacher's Multi-ROM to work with the Student's Book or with the Big Book Builder.

what people are doing.

1 Read the e-mail invitation to Kathy.

To ...   kathy@bouncemail.com

From ...   lucy@bouncemail.com

Hi Kathy,

It's my birthday today! I'm nine! Please come to my party. Jack is designing the posters. Fred is decorating the room. It looks fantastic! Angela is preparing the party food. She's making pizza and Jello! I'm making the decorations. What are you doing? Are you watching television? Are you eating a hamburger?

See you soon,

Lucy

2 Write an e-mail invitation to a friend for your birthday.

To ...

From ...

Hi (students' own answers) ,

_____

_____

_____

_____

_____.

_____,

_____

1 Listen and point. Say the words.

Track 38

eyes	ears	mouth	nose

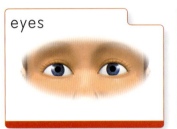 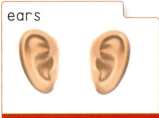 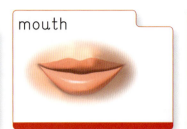 

eyebrows	teeth	hair	cheeks

2 Label the party mask.

1 hair

2 eyes

3 nose

4 mouth

5 eyebrows

6 ears

7 cheeks

8 teeth

Vocabulary presentation

Materials: track 38, a sheet of paper for each student, colored pencils, Big Book Builder 2 pages 18 and 19

Lesson objectives: Learn vocabulary about facial features

New vocabulary: *eyes, ears, mouth, nose, eyebrows, teeth, hair, cheeks*

1 Bounce into action!

- Explain to students that you are going to discuss facial features.
- Elicit from them all the words they know relating to parts of the body.
- Write their suggestions on the board.

2 Exercise 1

Listen and point. Say the words.

- Point to the pictures in the book and say *Listen and point*.
- Play track 38 and get students to point to the pictures as they hear them on the track.
- Say *Say the words*. Play the track again and press the pause button after each word so students can repeat the words together.
- Point to the features on your own face and have students imitate you and say the words.

3 Exercise 2

Label the party mask.

- Ask students to look at the mask and fill in the missing words.
- Go around the room helping and encouraging them to say the words as they are writing them.

Optional Activity:

Big Book Builder 2 pages 18 and 19, *The Concert*. Do the activities suggested on pages xi to xix of this book.

4 Bounce on!

1 Hand a sheet of paper to each student. Give them the following instructions and encourage them to follow them. Say *Draw a face. / Draw two big green eyes. / Draw one big ear and one small ear. / Draw a nose. / Color the nose purple. / Draw a big mouth. / Color the mouth orange*, etc. (10 minutes)

2 Play *Tic-tac-toe*. Draw a 3-by-3 grid. In each cell, draw one of the facial features. Divide the class into two groups: one team will be the Xs and the other the Os. Taking turns, ask each group to choose a square and say the word for the picture correctly. If they say the word correctly, they can place their mark on the grid. If they do not say it correctly, the drawing passes to the other team. The purpose of the game is to mark three cells in a row. The first team to have three marks in a row wins. (5 – 10 minutes)

Write the following task instruction on the board and ask students to copy it in the space provided:

"Follow the instructions. Make a mask."

Multi-ROM task   Student's Multi-ROM

Ask students to complete the Unit 8 Lesson 5 activity on the Student's Multi-ROM to review the vocabulary they have learned.

Interactive presentation. Use the Teacher's Multi-ROM to work with the Student's Book or with the Big Book Builder.

Lesson 6

Grammar presentation

Materials: track 39, cardboard, wool, colored pencils or pens

Lesson objectives:	Learn to ask and answer questions about facial features
Vocabulary review:	Facial features
New grammar:	*Are you coloring the eyes?* *Yes, we are. / No, we aren't.*

1 Bounce into action!

- Check that students have completed and understood the task in the Home Study section on page 100. (Answers: p.168)
- Point to your eyes and say *Eyes*. Point to your mouth and wait for students to say *Mouth*. Encourage them to touch their mouths as they are answering. Continue practicing all the new vocabulary words in the same way.
- Vary the order and speed at which you say the words.

2 Exercise 1

Listen and draw.

- Look and talk about the picture with the students.
- Explain to them that they are going to listen to a number of questions and answers; they must listen carefully as they are then to draw the corresponding pictures.
- Say *Listen* and play track 39.
- Play the track again and stop it after each answer to allow students to repeat it and then draw the picture.
- Play the track for the third time and check the students' work.
- Write *Today's grammar* on the board and ask students to copy it down.

> **Today's grammar**
> Are you coloring the eyes?
> Yes, we are. / No, we aren't.

Audioscript:

1 *Are you making the eyes?*
   Yes, we are.

2 *Now are you painting the eyebrows?*
   No, we aren't. We're painting the cheeks.

3 *Are you drawing the nose?*
   Yes, we are.

4 *Are you pasting on the teeth?*
   No, we aren't. We're pasting on the hair.

5 *Are you cutting out the ears?*
   Yes, we are.

6 *Are you painting the mouth?*
   Yes, we are.
   Are you painting it blue?
   No, we aren't. We're painting it purple.

3 Bounce back. Match the verbs with the correct nouns. (Review activity)

- Ask some of the students to read the words for the whole class.
- Have students match each verb to the correct noun.

4 Bounce on!

1 Say *Let's make a mask*. Divide the class into five groups. Give some cardboard and wool to each group to allow them to make a mask. Ask them to color and use wool for the hair. Encourage them to say the facial features as they are making the mask. Decorate the room with the masks. (10 – 15 minutes)

2 While the class is making their masks, ask the groups to ask their friends working on the other tables *Are you sticking on the hair? / Are you drawing the eyebrows?* The students from the other tables should answer *Yes, we are* or *No, we aren't*. (5 – 10 minutes)

> **Interactive presentation.** Use the Teacher's Multi-ROM to work with the Student's Book or with the Big Book Builder.

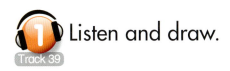 Listen and draw.

Track 39

Today's grammar

Are you coloring the eyes?
Yes, we are. / No, we aren't.

(students' own answers)

Bounce back

to Unit 7 Match the verbs with the correct nouns.

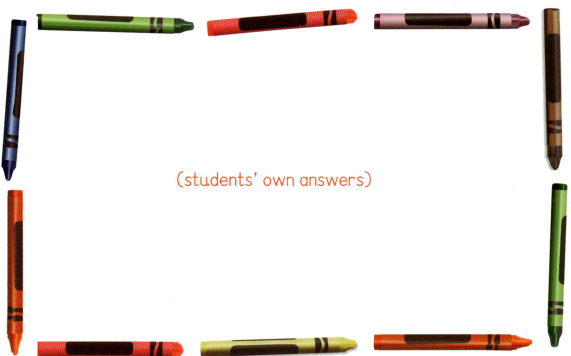

1	pour	the food
2	set	the dishes
3	wash	the drinks
4	serve	the table

Listen and read. *The best mask.*

Track 40

1

"What are you doing?" asks Mom.
"We're making masks for the mask competition at the party," says Judy.
"I want to win first prize," says Nathan.

2

"I'm coloring my mask pink, Mom," says Judy.
"I'm painting my mask green," says Nathan.

3

"Are you wearing your new black pants to the party?" asks Mom.
"No, I'm not. I'm wearing my green pajamas," says Nathan.
"Green pajamas! But Nathan… !"

4

"First prize goes to Nathan for his beautiful alien mask and his alien costume," says Mr. Pye.
"But… they are his pajamas!" says Judy.

 Describe Nathan's mask.

The eye is (students' own answers) _____.

66

Lesson 7

Read a story

Materials: track 40

Lesson objectives:	Listen to and read a story
	Write a sentence describing Nathan's mask
Vocabulary review:	Facial features

Bounce into action!

- Look at the pictures with students and tell them that they are going to listen to a story.
- Ask them to say what they think the story will be about.
- Discuss their suggestions and write some of their ideas on the board.

Exercise 1

 Listen and read. *The best mask.*

- Say *Listen* and play track 40. Encourage students to point to the pictures as they are mentioned on the story.
- Ask them to say what the story is about. Point to the ideas on the board and check any similarities to the story they have just listened to.
- Talk about the actions of the students and discuss what they are wearing to Nathan's party.
- Read the story again with the students. Ask a few of them to read the story by role-playing the different people in the story.

Exercise 2

Describe Nathan's mask.

- Ask questions to students to encourage them to describe Nathan's mask. Ask *What color is the eye? / Is the nose big or small?*, etc.
- Ask students to write a sentence to describe the mask.
- Go around the room helping them.

Bounce on!

1 Review the story's dialogue with the students. Divide the class into groups of four students and ask them to role-play the story. Have some of the groups come to the front and act out the story for the class. (10 minutes)

2 Draw an outline of a face on the board. Have one student come to the front. Ask them to draw the eyes. Then ask them to say a sentence with this word. Continue in this way using all the facial features. (10 – 15 minutes)

Multi-ROM task Student's Multi-ROM

Ask the students to listen to the story *The best mask*, track 40, at home until they can perform a role-play during the next class.

Interactive presentation. Use the Teacher's Multi-ROM to work with the Student's Book or with the Big Book Builder.

unit 8

Lesson 8

Bounce around: Civics

Materials: track 40, pictures of typical costumes, important festivals and handicrafts from other countries and from your own country, sheets of paper, colored pencils, Assessment Pack pages 4, 5 and 31

Lesson objectives: Learn through culture
Encourage a respectful attitude through the traditions and customs of your own country
Review the vocabulary learned during the unit
Vocabulary expansion

New vocabulary: *culture, costume, handicraft, festival, country*

1 Bounce into action!

- Play track 40. Listen to the story *The best mask*, and then ask students to come to the front and act out the story in groups of four.

2 Exercise 1

Read about culture. Circle the correct answer for each picture. Each country or region has its own customs and traditions. Their handicrafts, typical dress and dances are all different.

- Show the pictures of typical costumes, a festival and handicraft from a country. Ask students if they know the name of the country. Do the same thing with other pictures.
- Read the information all together. Talk to the students about the meaning of the word *culture*.
- Ask students to circle the correct answer.

3 Exercise 2

Draw a picture of a typical costume, handicraft or festival in your country.

- Place the pictures of a typical costume, handicraft or festival in your country on the board.

- Discuss with students the meaning of the pictures. Tell them what these symbols mean and what they represent for their country.
- Discuss with students the importance of respecting them.
- Ask students to choose the one they like the best and draw it in their books.
- Form pairs and have the students explain why they drew their picture.

4 Exercise 3

Talk about a cultural event.

- Ask students to talk about a cultural event in their country. Go around the room encouraging and helping the students.

5 Bounce on!

1 Ask students to compare typical costumes, handicrafts and festivals of their own and another country using a table. Encourage them to find the similarities and differences. Ask a few students to come to the front and explain their table. (5 – 10 minutes)

2 Ask students to write sentences about typical costumes, festivals and handicrafts in their country. (5 – 10 minutes)

Language Assessment: Photocopy the language assessment sheet on page 31 of the Assessment Pack. Give each student a copy to complete in order to check what they have learned over the course of the unit.

Self Assessment: Photocopy the self assessment sheet on page 4 of the Assessment Pack. Give a copy to each student for them to complete on their own. Offer help where necessary.

Global Assessment: Complete the global assessment on page 5 of the Assessment Pack. Check whether the objectives set out at the start of the unit were achieved by your students. Keep a record to refer back to in coming units.

Interactive presentation. Use the Teacher's Multi-ROM to work with the Student's Book or with the Big Book Builder.

Bounce around: Civics

1 Read about culture. Circle the correct answer for each picture. Each country or region has its own customs and traditions. Their handicrafts, typical dress and dances are all different.

(handicrafts)

handicrafts

handicrafts

typical dress

typical dress

(typical dress)

dance

(dance)

dance

2 Draw a picture of a typical costume, handicraft or festival in your country.

3 Talk about a cultural event.

Our town has a festival every year.

Talk about

 1 Listen and point. Say the words.
Track 41

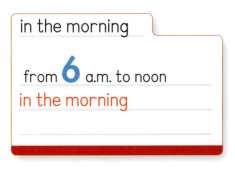

in the morning

from **6** a.m. to noon
in the morning
_____

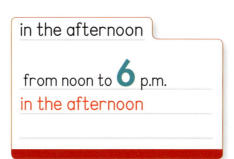

in the afternoon

from noon to **6** p.m.
in the afternoon
_____

in the evening

from **6** p.m. to **9** p.m.
in the evening
_____

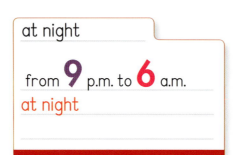

at night

from **9** p.m. to **6** a.m.
at night
_____

at noon

12 o'clock in the day
at noon
_____

early

early
_____

late

late
_____

at midnight

12 o'clock at night
at midnight
_____

 2 Write the words in exercise 1.

unit 9

Vocabulary presentation

Materials: track 41, cards, Activity Resource Book page 19, colored pencils, glue

Lesson objectives: Learn vocabulary about times of the day

New vocabulary: *in the morning, in the afternoon, in the evening, at night, at noon, at midnight, early, late*

Global assessment indicators
a Student works well in teams
b Student presents work with care
c Student respects classroom rules
d Student is interested in learning

1 Bounce into action!

- Describe to students a typical day in your life. Tell them what time you get up, what you do during the morning, afternoon and at night and discuss the time you go to sleep.
- Ask them to tell you what they do during the course of a day. Encourage them to say what they do in the morning, afternoon and at night.

2 Exercise 1

Listen and point. Say the words.

track 41
- Point to the pictures in the book and say *Listen and point*.
- Play track 41. Have students point out the pictures as they are mentioned on the track.
- Say *Say the words*. Play the track again and press the pause button after each word so students can repeat them together.

3 Exercise 2

Write the words in exercise 1.

- Ask students to write down the words.
- Go around the room helping and encouraging the students to say the words while they are writing them.

4 Word window (optional activity)

- Ask students to open their Activity Resource Book to page 19. Have them color in the clock and write the new words. Encourage students to cut out the cuckoo clock and the pendulum, and then show them how to hang it from the clock.
- Divide the class into pairs. Students are to take turns saying the parts of the day and point to the corresponding words on the clock's pendulum.
- Go around the room helping the pairs with their pronunciation and checking they are working properly.

5 Bounce on!

1 Write the new words and phrases in large letters on strips of card and place them around the room. Ask students to stand up. Say *In the evening*. Students must point to the phrase indicated. Continue in the same way changing the order and the speed. (5 – 10 minutes)

2 Say the new words or phrases and mime an action for each one. Say *Midnight* and pretend to be sleeping. Say the words in any order and encourage students to do the corresponding action. (5 – 10 minutes)

Multi-ROM task Student's Multi-ROM

Ask students to complete the Unit 9 Lesson 1 activity on the Student's Multi-ROM to review the vocabulary they have learned.

Interactive presentation. Use the Teacher's Multi-ROM to work with the Student's Book or with the Big Book Builder.

unit 9

Lesson 2

Grammar presentation

Materials: tracks 42 and 43, Big Book Builder 2 pages 20 and 21

Lesson objectives:	Learn to ask and say the time
Vocabulary review:	Parts of the day
New grammar:	*What time is it? It's two o'clock.*

1 Bounce into action!

- Say the words or phrases of the new vocabulary in any order and encourage students to do the actions.
- Do the actions and have students say the phrases.
- Change the order of the words and actions.

2 Exercise 1

Listen and write the times under the clocks.

- Draw a clock on the board. Ask *What time is it?* Point to the hands and say *It's three o'clock.* Model the new structure again and have students repeat it first together and then individually. Change the hands on the clock and continue in the same way.
- Write *Today's grammar* on the board and ask students to copy it down.

> **Today's grammar**
> What time is it?   It's . . . o'clock.

- Look at the clocks in the book with the students. Play track 42 and encourage them to write the time indicated.
- Play the track again and use the pause button to give students enough time to write down the times.

3 Exercise 2

Draw the hands on the clocks.

- Ask students to draw the hands on the clocks.
- Go around the room helping and encouraging them.

4 Exercise 3

Say the times.

- Divide the class into groups. Ask students to look at the clocks and then take turns asking and answering questions about the time.

5 Exercise 4

Listen and check.

- Ask one of the students to read the instruction aloud. Play track 43 and encourage them to check their work.
- Play the track again and correct the work with the students.

> **Optional Activity:**
> **Big Book Builder 2** pages 20 and 21, *The Time.* Do the activities suggested on pages xi to xix of this book.

6 Bounce on!

1 Divide the class into two teams. Draw a number of clocks on the board. Say a time of the day and get several students from each team to draw the hands. If the student draws the correct time, he/she will win a point for his/her team. (5 – 10 minutes)

2 Have several students come to the front to write the time below each clock. The rest of the class is to say the time all together. (5 – 10 minutes)

Home Study
page 101

Write the following task instructions on the board and ask students to copy them in the space provided:

"Draw various times on the clocks. Write the correct time, using the ones in exercise 1 to help you."

Interactive presentation. Use the Teacher's Multi-ROM to work with the Student's Book or with the Big Book Builder.

Listen and write the times under the clocks.

Track 42

Today's grammar

What time is it?
It's 2 o'clock.

unit **9** LESSON **2**

1 It's one o'clock .

3 It's four o'clock .

5 It's five o'clock .

2 It's nine o'clock .

4 It's ten o'clock .

6 It's noon .

 Draw the hands on the clocks.

1 It's 2 o'clock.

3 It's 3 o'clock.

5 It's 6 o'clock.

2 It's 7 o'clock.

4 It's 8 o'clock.

6 It's 11 o'clock.

 Say the times.

 Listen and check.

Track 43

Home Study page 101 **69**

1 Write sentences about Wilomena the Witch and Wilfred the Wizard.

Today's grammar

It's noon.
Wilomena is playing with her friends.

1

It's noon.

Wilomena is playing with her friends .

2

It's 8 o'clock in the morning.

Wilfred is making a snack .

3

It's 6 o'clock in the evening.

Wilomena is eating .

4

It's 2 o'clock in the afternoon.

Wilfred is cooking .

5

It's midnight.

Wilomena is sleeping .

6

It's 10 o'clock at night.

Wilfred is reading .

Lesson 3

Grammar presentation

Materials: Big Book Builder 2 pages 20 and 21, sheets of paper, colored pencils

Lesson objectives: Write sentences about Wilfred and Wilomena

Vocabulary review: Parts of the day

New grammar: *It's eight o'clock. Wilfred is in the park playing football.*

1 Bounce into action!

- Check that students have completed and understood the task in the Home Study section on page 101. (Answers: p.168)
- Write the words and phrases of the review vocabulary on one side of the board. Point to the pictures one after another and have students say them.
- Draw a clock on the board. Draw the hands, underline one of the phrases on the side of the board and ask *What time is it?* Encourage students to answer *It's four o'clock in the afternoon.*
- Change the hands on the clock and underline one of the other vocabulary phrases and ask the time. Encourage students to answer all together. Continue in this way until all the vocabulary has been reviewed.

2 Exercise 1

Write sentences about Wilomena the Witch and Wilfred the Wizard.

- Look at the pictures of Wilfred and Wilomena with the students.
- Point to the first picture of Wilomena and encourage students to look at the time indicated. Say *It's noon and Wilomena is playing with her friends.* Have students repeat the structure several times together.
- Point to the first picture of Wilfred and follow the same steps.
- Point to each of the pictures and ask students to say the sentences.
- Write *Today's grammar* on the board and ask students to copy it down.

Today's grammar

It's noon.

Wilomena is playing with her friends.

Wilfred is drinking milk.

- Have one student come to the front and write the first sentence of the exercise on the board.
- Have the students write the sentences in their books.
- Go around the room helping them to form the sentences.

Optional Activity:

Big Book Builder 2 pages 20 and 21, *The Time.* Do the activities suggested on pages xi to xix of this book.

3 Bounce on!

1 Divide the class into two teams. Draw a clock on the board. Have one student come to the front and ask him/her to draw the hands on the clock asking *What time is it?* Get a student from the other team to come to the front and ask him/her to write the time shown. If they write the sentence correctly, they will win a point for their team. Have two other students come to the front and follow the same steps. The team with the most points is the winner. (10 minutes)

2 Hand out sheets of paper. Ask students to draw what they do at each time of the day and write the time. Ask a few students to come to the front and show their pictures and talk about them. Emphasize the parts of the day and the times. (15 minutes)

Interactive presentation. Use the Teacher's Multi-ROM to work with the Student's Book or with the Big Book Builder.

unit **9**

Lesson 4

Song presentation

Materials: track 44, a sheet of paper for each student, a ball, Activity Resource Book page 30, Big Book Builder 2 pages 20 and 21

Lesson objectives:	Learn the song *What time is it?* Discuss your activities at various times of the day
Vocabulary review:	Parts of the day
Grammar review:	*What time is it? It's three o'clock.*

① Bounce into action!

- Draw a clock on the board. Draw the hands and ask the class *What time is it?* Encourage them to answer together.
- Erase the hands and ask a student to draw another time of day. Encourage him/her to ask *What time is it?* The other students should answer with the correct time.
- Get other students to come to the front and continue asking and answering questions about the time.

② Exercise 1

Sing the song: *What time is it?*

- Tell students they are going to listen to a song. Play track 44 and mime the actions of the song.
- Play the track again and encourage students to tell the time by counting on their fingers and performing the actions.
- Model the song's lines and get students to repeat the lines together.
- Play the track again and sing the song together.
- Ask students to open their Activity Resource Book to page 30 and do the activities.

③ Exercise 2

Talk time. Say what you are doing at these times. Ask your friends.

- Look at the clocks with the students and ask *What time is it?* Encourage them to answer together.
- Ask a few students what activities they normally do at that time. Encourage them to say *It's three o'clock. I'm playing soccer.*
- Divide the class into pairs and get them to take turns asking and answering questions about the activities they normally do at various times.

> **Optional Activity:**
> **Big Book Builder 2** pages 20 and 21, *The Time.* Do the activities suggested on pages xi to xix of this book.

④ Bounce on!

1 Students are to sit in a circle. Pass the ball and say *It's one o'clock.* One of the students passes the ball to the next student and says *It's two o'clock.* Continue in this way until you say *Stop.* The student holding the ball then comes to the center of the circle and mimes the activity he/she normally does at that time and then says it aloud.
(10 minutes)

2 Hand a sheet of paper to each student. Dictate the phrase *It's seven o'clock in the morning* three times and ask them to write it down. Say some of the other phrases three times. Get the students to exchange their sheet with a friend. Correct the phrases with the students. (10 minutes)

Home Study page 102

Write the following task instructions on the board and ask students to copy them in the space provided:

"Draw yourself in each box doing the activities. Write sentences about the time when you do these activities."

Multi-ROM task Student's Multi-ROM

Ask the students to listen to the song *What time is it?*, track 44, at home until they have memorized it.

Interactive presentation. Use the Teacher's Multi-ROM to work with the Student's Book or with the Big Book Builder.

1 Track 44

Sing the song: What time is it?

It's 1 o'clock, 2 o'clock, 3 o'clock, wow!
What time is it? Tell me now.

It's 4 o'clock, 5 o'clock, 6 o'clock, stop!
What time is it? Look at the clock.

It's 7 o'clock, 8 o'clock, 9 o'clock, wait!
What time is it? It's very late.

It's 10 o'clock, 11 o'clock, 12 o'clock, hey!
What time is it? Look, it's noon. Yeah!

It's 1 o'clock, 2 o'clock, 3 o'clock, wow!
What time is it? Tell me now.

It's 4 o'clock, 5 o'clock, 6 o'clock, stop!
What time is it? Look at the clock.

It's 7 o'clock, 8 o'clock, 9 o'clock, wait!
What time is it? It's very late.

It's 10 o'clock, 11 o'clock, 12 o'clock, right!
What time is it? Look, it's midnight.

2 Say what you are doing at these times. Ask your friends.

Talk time

It's 3 o'clock. What are you doing?

 1 Listen and point. Say the words.

Track 45

have breakfast

have lunch

have dinner

get up

do the chores

recess

read a story

go to bed

 2 Look at the picture clues and write the words.

1  have lunch

2  go to bed

3  have breakfast

4  get up

5  do the chores

6  recess

7 read a story

8  have dinner

Lesson 5

Vocabulary presentation

Materials: tracks 44 and 45

Lesson objectives: Learn and write vocabulary about daily activities

New vocabulary: *have breakfast, have lunch, have dinner, get up, do the chores, recess, read a story, go to bed*

1 Bounce into action!

- Check that students have completed and understood the task in the Home Study section on page 102. (Answers: p.168)
- Play track 44. Sing the song *What time is it?*
- Divide the class into eight groups. Each group is to sing two lines of the song. Point to the groups in the correct order and sing the song.
- Point to the groups randomly and sing the song in any order.

2 Exercise 1

Listen and point. Say the words.

- Point to the pictures of the new words and say *Listen and point*. Play track 45 and get students to point to the pictures as they hear them on the track.
- Say *Say the words*. Play the track again and press the pause button after each word or phrase so students can repeat them.
- Point to the pictures and ask students to say the phrases or words of the new vocabulary individually.

3 Exercise 2

Look at the picture clues and write the words.

- Ask students to look at the pictures. Encourage them to decipher the clues provided in each picture and write the phrase or word indicated for each one.
- Go around the room helping and encouraging them while they are working.

4 Bounce on!

1  Do a short dictation of the sentences using the words of the vocabulary seen during this lesson. Then ask students to draw pictures relating to the sentences. (10 minutes)

2 Write the words and phrases of the new vocabulary on the board, but with the words jumbled up: *fbrstaeka veah* (*have breakfast*). Divide the class into groups. Students are to work in teams to put the letters in the correct order and write the words correctly. The first group managing to write all the phrases correctly is the winner. (10 minutes)

Multi-ROM task Student's Multi-ROM

Ask students to complete the Unit 9 Lesson 5 activity on the Student's Multi-ROM to review the vocabulary they have learned.

Interactive presentation. Use the Teacher's Multi-ROM to work with the Student's Book or with the Big Book Builder.

unit 9

Materials: track 46

Lesson objectives:	Learn to say it's time to do an activity
Vocabulary review:	Daily activities
New grammar:	*It's time for lunch. / It's time to go to bed.*

❶ Bounce into action!

- Write the phrases and words of the vocabulary on cards and place them at various places around the room.
- Say one of the vocabulary phrases or words. Students are to point to the word and do the corresponding action.
- Continue in this way until all the vocabulary has been reviewed.

❷ Exercise 1

track 46

Listen and complete the clock faces.
Write sentences.

- Draw an alarm clock on the board. Pretend to wake up and say *It's six o'clock in the morning. It's time to get up.* Repeat the sentences and drill them together and then individually.
- Write *Today's grammar* on the board and ask students to copy it down.

> **Today's grammar**
>
> It's time | for lunch.
> | to go to bed.

- Explain that they must listen carefully and complete the clock faces. Play track 46 and stop it after each section to allow students to draw the hands.

Audioscript:
7 gongs: It's time for breakfast.
10 gongs: OK, children, it's time for recess.
1 gong: Wash your hands! Lunch is ready, children.
8 gongs: I'm serving dinner. Come on!

❸ Exercise 2

Complete the sentences.

- Read the sentences with students. Encourage them to suggest activities they are normally doing at those times.
- Ask one of the students to come to the front and write the first sentence on the board.
- Ask them to complete the sentences on their own.

❹ Bounce back! Read and color.
(Review activity)

- Ask a few students to read the sentences aloud. Encourage the class to point to the clown's features as they are mentioned.
- Ask them to color in the clown. Go around the room correcting their work.

❺ Bounce on!

1 Divide the class into groups. Write the following on the board: *seven morning It's the o'clock in breakfast time It's for.* Students are to put the words in the correct order and write the sentences. (5 – 10 minutes)

2 Divide the class into pairs. Ask them to draw clock faces showing different times. Students are to take turns saying the time and what they do at that time: *It's ten o'clock in the morning. It's time to do the chores.* (10 minutes)

Home Study page 103

Write the following task instructions on the board and ask students to copy them in the space provided:
"Put the words in the correct order. Tell the time."

Interactive presentation. Use the Teacher's Multi-ROM to work with the Student's Book or with the Big Book Builder.

Listen and complete the clock faces. Write sentences.

Today's grammar

It's time for lunch.
It's time to go to bed.

 It's time for ___breakfast___.

3 It's time for ___lunch___.

 It's time for ___recess___.

4  It's time for ___dinner___.

2 Complete the sentences.

1 It's 6 o'clock in the morning.

It's time for ___getting up___.

2 It's 3 o'clock in the afternoon.

___It's time for recess___.

3 It's 7 o'clock in the evening.

___It's time to have dinner___.

4 It's 8 o'clock at night.

___It's time to go to bed___.

Bounce back

to Unit 8 Read and color.

His cheeks are red.

His hair is orange.

His eyes are blue.

And his teeth are, too!

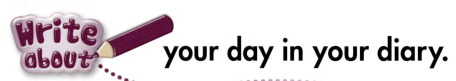 **your day in your diary.**

1 Read about Sam's day in his diary.

Sunday, September 28th

Today's Sunday. It's ____ .

It's ____ . I'm wearing my

____ and my ____ .

I'm in my ____ .

I'm doing my ____ . Mom is

calling me. "It's time for ____ .

It's time to ____ ."

2 Write about your day in your diary. Draw pictures.

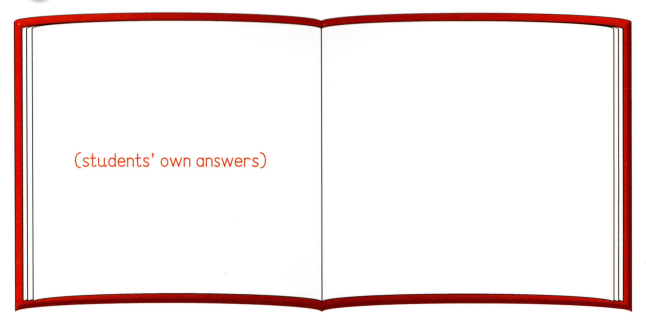

(students' own answers)

3 Ask your friends to read your story.

Lesson 7

Write about . . . your day in your diary.

Materials: track 44, colored pencils, a ball, music, Big Book Builder 2 pages 20 and 21

Lesson objectives:	Read and write a diary entry
Vocabulary review:	*Daily activities*
Grammar review:	*It's two o'clock. It's time to + verb / It's time for + noun*

1 Bounce into action!

- Check that students have completed and understood the task in the Home Study section on page 103. (Answers: p.168)
- Sing the song *What time is it?* Play track 44 if necessary.
- Get students to mime the actions of the song.

2 Exercise 1

Read about Sam's day in his diary.

- Read the text with the students. Encourage them to look at the pictures and guess the correct words using the clues.
- Talk about Sam's actions. Ask the following comprehension questions: *What day is it? / What time is it? / Is it raining? / What's Sam wearing? / Where is Sam? / What's he doing? / Why is Mom calling?*
- Read the text again. Ask a few students to read the sentences for the whole class, replacing the pictures with the correct words.

3 Exercise 2

Write about your day in your diary. Draw pictures.

- Explain to students that they are going to pretend to be writing a diary entry about their day.
- Write a model of a diary entry on the board with the students. One by one, read the sentences of Sam's diary and write similar sentences. Leave out a few words and get some students to come to the front and draw the corresponding pictures.

- Read the text they have just written and replace the drawings with the corresponding words.
- Ask students to write a similar text and draw the pictures in their books.
- Go around the room helping and encouraging them.

4 Exercise 3

Ask your friends to read your story.

- Play music and get students to take their books and walk around the room. When the music stops, they must sit down next to the closest person.
- Ask the pairs to take turns reading the diary entry of their partner. Go around helping the pairs with their pronunciation. Then switch the music back on and follow the same steps.

> **Optional Activity:**
>
> **Big Book Builder 2** pages 20 and 21, *The Time.* Do the activities suggested on pages xi to xix of this book.

5 Bounce on!

1 Divide the class into two teams. Get one member from each team to come to the front to write dashes instead of letters of one of the expressions of the new vocabulary. The other student must try to guess the missing letters. If he/she guesses one of the letters correctly, the other student must write the letter in the expression. If the letter is not in the expression, the other student is to draw part of the hangman. The team guessing the most words is the winner. (5 – 10 minutes)

2 Throw the ball to a student and say *It's two o'clock. It's time to...* and get them to complete the phrase. Continue in this way with other students, changing the times. (5 – 10 minutes)

> **Interactive presentation.** Use the Teacher's Multi-ROM to work with the Student's Book or with the Big Book Builder.

Lesson 8

Bounce around: Language

Materials: Assessment Pack pages 4, 5 and 32

Lesson objectives: Practice the unit's language
Integrate the new vocabulary with the vocabulary already learned

Vocabulary review: Daily activities, time

1 Bounce into action!

- Play *Bounce says!* Explain to students that you are going to say sentences. If the sentence starts with the phrase *Bounce says*, they must do the action. If it does not, they must not move. Say *Bounce says: have breakfast.* Students are to pretend to be having breakfast. Say *Do the chores.* Students are to remain motionless.

2 Exercise 1

Read about Steve and answer the question.

- Read the paragraph with the students.
- Ask the students what Steve has to do when he gets up. Then ask them how many hours Steve needs to get ready.
- Read and answer the question.

3 Exercise 2

Talk about your routine.

- Say *Let's talk about your routine!*
- Ask questions to students about what they do when they get up. Ask them if they do the same things as Steve, or if they do different things.
- Encourage them to use the vocabulary they have learned during the course.
- Involve as many students as possible.

4 Bounce on!

1 Divide the class in two. Give some cardboard and a pen to each group and tell them that they are to work in teams to write sentences about their routine when they get up. The team managing to write the most correct sentences will win. (10 minutes)

2 Sing the song *What time is it?* Encourage students to mime the actions of the song. (5 minutes)

Language Assessment: Photocopy the language assessment sheet on page 32 of the Assessment Pack. Give each student a copy to complete in order to check what they have learned over the course of the unit.

 Self Assessment: Photocopy the self assessment sheet on page 4 of the Assessment Pack. Give a copy to each student for them to complete on their own. Offer help where necessary.

Global Assessment: Complete the global assessment on page 5 of the Assessment Pack. Check whether the objectives set out at the start of the unit have been achieved by your students. Keep a record and assess students over the whole year.

Interactive presentation. Use the Teacher's Multi-ROM to work with the Student's Book or with the Big Book Builder.

1 Read about Steve and answer the question.

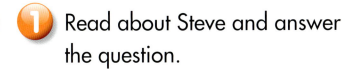

- Steve plays soccer on Saturdays.

- He needs to be at the class at 10.00.

- He needs an hour to get there.

- He needs an hour to meet a friend and do his homework.

- He needs half an hour to have breakfast and he needs half an hour to take a shower and get dressed.

What time does Steve need to get up?   <u>Seven o'clock</u>

2 Talk about your routine.

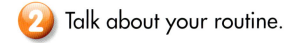
I get up at 6 o'clock.

Talk about

Home Study Worksheet Answers

Unit 1

 Exercise 1. first – 1st, second – 2nd, third – 3rd, fourth – 4th, fifth – 5th, sixth – 6th, seventh – 7th, eighth – 8th, ninth – 9th, tenth – 10th

 Exercise 1. **1** February **2** December **3** April **4** June **5** November

Exercise 2. ninth

 Exercise 1. **2** Halloween **3** Christmas **4** Easter **5** birthday

Exercise 2. The students decorate the card and write a sentence about the corresponding special day.

Unit 2

 Exercise 1. The students color in the picture.

Exercise 2. Denzel's wearing a T-shirt, shorts and sandals.

 Exercise 1. The students draw themselves wearing a blue sweater, orange pants and red shoes.

Exercise 2. The students complete the poem using their own words.

 Exercise 1. T-shirt, sandals, sweater, pants, dress, shoes, coat.

Exercise 2.

Exercise 3. Mona Monster is wearing a dress and sandals.

Unit 3

 Exercise 1. **2** cry **3** drink **4** play **5** talk **6** skate **7** eat **8** sing

Exercise 2. **1** He's drinking. **2** She's crying. **3** She's skating.

 Exercise 1. Toby Turtle is in the park. He's listening to music. He's singing. He isn't drinking soda and he isn't eating a hamburger. He isn't playing baseball. He's laughing.

 Exercise 1. The students read the text.

Exercise 2. The students draw, paint and cut out a flower. Stick the flower in the box.

Home Study Worksheet Answers

Unit 4

Exercise 1. The students join the numbers together to complete the picture. Complete the sentence: The monkeys are eating ice cream cones.

Exercise 2. The monkeys are eating. The dogs are swimming.

Exercise 1. The students design the postcard with people doing typical activities.

Exercise 2. (examples) **1** They are making sandcastles. **2** They are sleeping on the sand. **3** They are buying ice cream cones.

Exercise 1. **1** aren't **2** aren't **3** are **4** are **5** are **6** aren't

Exercise 2. **1** F **2** T **3** F **4** T

Unit 5

Exercise 1. The students color in the television and draw their favorite program.

Exercise 2. They should complete the sentence with the name of their favorite program.

Exercise 1. **2** I'm not riding my bicycle. I'm doing my homework. **3** I'm not making a snack. I'm watering the plants. **4** I'm not cleaning my room. I'm calling my friends.

Exercise 2. The students draw themselves and write sentences about what they are doing.

Exercise 1. **1** thirty-seven – 37, sixty-five – 65, twenty-six – 26, ninety-three – 93, forty-nine – 49, seventy-eight – 78

Exercise 2. forty-nine, sixty-five, seventy-eight, ninety-three

Exercise 3. **1** forty **2** sixty-six **3** eighty

Unit 6

Exercise 1. **2** No, it isn't. **3** No, it isn't. **4** Yes, he is.

Exercise 2. No, she isn't.

Exercise 1 & 2. **2** help **3** take care of **4** fix **5** examine **6** drive **7** answer **8** operate on

Exercise 1. **1** (The students draw a lady with an umbrella.)

2 (The students draw a bear eating a banana.)

3 (The students draw a hippopotamus driving a car.)

4 (The students draw a dog playing with a ball.)

Home Study Worksheet Answers

Unit 7

 Exercise 1.   lemonade   French fries   hamburger   jello   milk   pizza   apple pie   salad

Exercise 2.   food: French fries, hamburger, jello, pizza, apple pie, salad
drink: lemonade, milk

 Exercise 1.   The students are eating hamburgers and jello.

Exercise 2.   No, they aren't.

Exercise 3.   The students write another coded message.

 Exercise 1.   **1** Are they drinking milk or soda?

2 Are they eating French fries or sausages?

Exercise 2.   **1** They are drinking milk.   **2** They are eating sausages.

Unit 8

 Exercise 1.   **1** Petra is having a party.   **2** On Saturday   **3** She is eight on Saturday.

Exercise 2.   The students draw their fancy dress costume for the party.

 Exercise 1.   The students draw themselves and three friends.

Exercise 2.   The students choose the task that each person is to do and write the sentences below each picture.

Exercise 3.   The students answer the questions about themselves.

 Exercise 1.   The students follow the instructions. The mask must have brown eyes, an orange mouth, green skin and

two black eyebrows.

Unit 9

 Exercise 1.   The students draw the time on each of the six clocks.

Exercise 2.   The students write the time on each clock. Starting their sentences with It's...

 Exercise 1.   The students draw themselves doing the following activities:

1 reading a story   **2** going to bed   **3** having breakfast   **4** doing the chore

Exercise 2.   The students write sentences describing the time they normally do each activity in exercise 1.

Exercise 1.   **1** get up **2** have breakfast **3** have dinner **4** go to bed

Exercise 2.   The students answer the questions about themselves.